My Life With
NOBI

A Guide for a Successful Life

James Washington

My Life With NOBI

Copyright © 2024 by James Washington

ISBN: 978-1639458578 (sc)
ISBN: 978-1639458585 (e)

All rights reserved. No part of this publication may be reproduced, distributed, or transmitted in any form or by any means, including photocopying, recording, or other electronic or mechanical methods, without the prior written permission of the publisher and/or the author, except in the case of brief quotations embodied in critical reviews and other noncommercial uses permitted by copyright law.

The views expressed in this book are solely those of the author and do not necessarily reflect the views of the publisher, and the publisher hereby disclaims any responsibility for them.

Writers' Branding
(877) 608-6550
www.writersbranding.com
media@writersbranding.com

Table of Contents

Preface v

Chapter 1: Our Meeting 1
Chapter 2: Korean War Years 7
Chapter 3: Marriages, Visa, and Home to the States 17
Chapter 4: Our First Stateside Assignment....................................... 21
Chapter 5: Moving to Colorado 27
Chapter 6: Going to Germany 31
Chapter 7: Our stay at Fort Ord 41
Chapter 8: Tour in France 57
Chapter 9: Our stay at Fort Carson 77
Chapter 10: My tour in Vietnam.. 85
Chapter 11: The Medical Evacuation Chain 95
Chapter 12: My Second Tour at Fort Ord 103
Chapter 13: Emptying Nest.. 115
Chapter 14: Our Travels (Atlantic City and Washington DC) 123
Chapter 15: A Sad Time for our Daughter 129
Chapter 16: Our Golden Wedding Anniversary 133
Chapter 17: Cruise to the Bahamas.. 135
Chapter 18: Travel With My Parents 139
Chapter 19: More of our Travels... 155
Chapter 20: Robert and Barbara's Silver Anniversary 175
Chapter 21: The last of…... 179
Chapter 22: Love Beyond the Grave 185

Preface

Nobuko Dodo was born on January 6, 1928 at Hokadate, Hokkaido Japan. I was born on March 11, 1931 at Little Rock, Arkansas. The chance of us meeting, falling in love and raising a family was remote due to the distance and the circumstances of our lives at the time. World War II had ended only two years earlier and Japan was in shambles. Just prior to the end of the war, I had no intention of having a military career. I had completed high school and began attending college. It is my belief that God had everything to do with this union.

It all started when a few of my friends and I were bored over the summer months and would go to the Recruiting Main Station and pretend we wanted to join the military. We would spend the day undergoing all the tests, both physical and mental, until it was time to take the oath of enlistment. We would then leave and go home without signing the oath form. In addition I was too young so I had to have my parent's consent. After starting college at the end of the summer months, the recruiters were very short on filling their quota and asked us to help them. My friend Wallace Warren and I decided that this would be another thrill and we could come home and attend college after a short tour in the Army. I had to hurry and get my parent's permission affidavit completed in order to be sworn in and leave on the train on that day. After completing basic training, I was sent to Japan. This improved my chances of meeting the love of my life, but I did not know it then. The Army had rules and regulations regarding our conduct with the people of Japan. We could show no affection toward a Japanese female. We could not even hold hands with one. Also the customs of Japan at that time dictated that the woman could not walk on the even plane with a man. She had to remain at least one step behind him. We were not allowed to eat or drink anything outside of a military base.

When we did meet, we were two lost souls. Neither of us was happy nor content until we found each other; although I always believed that God gave her to me. When I was growing up, I was often disciplined for fighting while Nobi was just the opposite. Yet, our lives together lasted over a span of sixty- two years, until her death on January 21, 2011. Before her death, she told me that she had had a wonderful life here with me and that if she had not met me and had stayed in Japan, she would have been dead long ago. She was the love of my life and I will hold her in my heart forever.

My wife was not one who loved expensive clothes and jewelry. When I first retired from the army, my retirement pay was less than half of my pay on active duty and my pay at GAC Finance was nothing to crow about. One of my duties was to pick up the mail at the post office for which I was given a weekly stipend. On occasions I saved part of my lunch money and the small check I received for getting the mail, I went to Monterey after work to a woman's clothing store called "Mode O'Day" and purchased a $9.00 dress (I knew her size). She was so thrilled when I brought it home to her; her face lit up like stars. It pleased me so much to see her reaction to such a costless gift. On the other hand, when I started to be paid "the big bucks" and we had more money than we needed, a son of one of our neighbors owned a jewelry store. He had a pair of diamond ear rings for sale that original cost $4000.00 but he told me that I could buy then for $975.00. I told him then that I knew he had to earn money since he was in business for that purpose but he told me that there was plenty of profit contained in the price. My wife wore these expensive ear rings a total of two times before she said that they hurt her ears. They were placed in the safe then and to this day, they are still there. I loved her so much that I thought she should have nice things so I brought from the jewelry store of another friend a fresh water pearl necklace with an 18 carat gold chain that now accompanies the diamond ear rings in the safe. I learned my lesson after this and always let her pick her own jewelry which I am sure did not cost much.

I spent my whole life with this woman and loved her every minute of it. She captured my heart from the beginning and retained it even after she departed this earth. I hope that God will see fit to allow me to see her again in the afterlife or wherever she is now.

MY LIFE WITH NOBI

BY: JAMES W. WASHINGTON

Chapter 1

OUR MEETING

Before I begin the story of my life with Nobuko, I want to explain why I happen to be in the place where the chance meeting took place. I was a private first class in the army stationed in Japan and was assigned to the 76th Antiaircraft Artillery Automatic Weapons Battalion (Self Propelled). There was a fierce rivalry with the 933rd Antiaircraft Artillery Battalion (Towed), that we were always fighting. Shortly after being moved from Yokohama, Japan because of these fights, a club was established on one end of the post. This club was much too small for these two units in such a small space. Fights often broke out and lasted until the military police were called to quell the fighting. It was on a clear October night that one of these fights took place, however I happened not to be present at the club, but was nearby. As I was running to join in on the fighting to help my unit, I saw a young woman running away from the club toward the street. I was not paying too much attention to her as I was sped by on my quest to join in on the fighting, that I ran smack into her and knocked her down on the ground pretty hard. I kept on running for a few steps but then my conscience began telling me that it was a shitty thing to do, leaving her there on the ground, so I walked back, picked her up and said in a rough voice, "Why don't you watch where you are going".

Thus began my life with the woman with whom I would spend the next 62 years. After I helped her up from the ground, she said to me, "If you go down there, you will just get into trouble as the military police are already there". There was a big rock nearby, so we sat upon the rock and talked. We then exchanged names and I began to look her over, and began to like what I was seeing. She was 20 years old and I had not yet reached my 18th birthday. She thought she knew everything. As we sat on the rock, it was not yet dark but I could see that she glowed around the head and at this time, I knew that God had brought us together. I found out everything I could about her however I think I revealed more about myself that I received from her. In fact, as I thought about it later, I had found out next to nothing about her, but I was satisfied with what I did know. My army friends had been hazing me about not having a girlfriend so I thought this girl would do nicely. I had no idea that she would be my lifetime partner. As nighttime began to fall, we decided to go to her house and continue talking. At this time, we had not agreed to date or be an item.

Being young and from what I had experienced with other Japanese women, I thought for sure I would get to first base, if not hit a home run, but this was not the case. I did not even get a good night kiss when it was time for me to depart for camp. We had to be inside the gates of the camp at midnight. When I was in my bed, I could not help thinking about her and the next morning I put in for a pass so I could go see her. When I got to her house, I thought we would at least talk there, but this was not the case. She immediately said that we would be going to Yokohama because she wanted me to meet her guardian since her family lived too far away.

We went to the train station and took the train to Yokohama, then took another train to a small town by the name of Namamugi, and then on to a section of town where the houses were quite large for being Japanese house. Before we got to the house we were seeking, she told me that I had to have a small gift so we stopped in a place where there were stores where she picked out my gift (of course I paid). We proceeded to her guardian's house. I was also told that I was expected to eat anything that was put before me. I was leery about this because during this time we were not supposed to eat anything except in camp. There I met an elderly Japanese lady by name of Kazuko Yamanari. This was too much for me to say, so I called her Namamugi Obasan. After being introduced, nothing but Japanese was spoken and I understood very little of it. Later I learned that Nobi wanted someone bigger, stronger and older than I and that she thought I was too young and this was the reason for our visit. Somehow I won approval from Obasan. When we were ready to leave, Obasan pointed her finger at me and said, "Only this girl, only this girl".

The next evening when I came to her house, we immediately went on another trip to Yokohama, only this time we went to visit a doctor somewhere near the home of Namamugi Obasan. We were admitted to this house as though we were expected. The doctor had a wife and two daughters. Nobi and the doctor went into another room while I was left with the daughters. Soon the younger daughter disappeared and I was left with the older daughter. I immediately became aware that this was another test so when the older daughter wanted me to sit on the piano stool with her while she played it; I kept my hands to myself and refused to make anything that resembled a pass. Then Nobi and the doctor soon appeared and we left to return to Zama. Although she was considered my girlfriend, I had yet to do more than hold her hand, and even that I could not do in public because of army regulations.

The next day was Saturday, therefore we got off after the noon meal and I made a beeline to Nobi's house. This time there was no trip out of town. However we make a trip to an office building that had a sign reading "register". We went in and Nobi said something to the man in Japanese and when she finished, she told me to give him 20 yen. The man made an entry into a big book and we left. Later I learned that we were married according to Japanese law, but not recognized by the American authorities. Upon arrival back at her house, things were much different. She let me kiss her; hold her in my arms and that night we made love for the first time. I knew that I loved this woman and would spend the rest of my life with her, regardless of what might take place with the army. I knew that even if the army sent me home without her, I would find some way to either get her to America or I would come back to Japan for her.

Things went pretty well for us after then. I was promoted to corporal, and was made Company Clerk. This meant that we would have more money. We purchased things for our house like a bed so we would not have to sleep on the floor Japanese style. I don't know how it happened, but I no longer saw my friends like I did before Nobi came into my life. Some of it might have been that I was company clerk and spent most of the day with the first sergeant, from whom my friends stayed far away. I also noticed that the old Japanese men allowed me into their circles and I began to understand more of their language. I drank with them sometimes.

As we spent more and more time together I wanted her to have something that I either designed or made myself. A design of a dress came into my mind, so I drew it out on paper, at work, and obtained the right kind of material. We went to a dress maker in town and when I gave her my design; the dress maker told me that the dress should be made in two pieces, a skirt and blouse or jacket. Here I make one of my few mistakes, I forcefully said to make it as shown. The dress maker did as instructed. The finished product was very awkward getting into it, but I would not admit the dress maker was right. Nobi wore the dress but not nearly as much because it was hard to get into and if she was not careful, she would tear at the seams. I still would not admit I was wrong and have the dress made as the dress maker wanted in the first place. I still cherished the few times she did wear the dress.

A few months passed and everything was going great between us. I spent as much time as I could with her. A new army regulation came out that permitted us single soldiers to get overnight passes based on performance of duty. Since I was the company clerk, I could put my name on the list to get the overnight pass daily. After the first sergeant approved the list, I was the one who typed up the passes for the company commander's signature. Now I could spend more time with the woman that I loved. It also meant that I did not have to get back to camp before midnight.

It is now June 1950 and the Korean War had started. The high command thought that we should protect the airfields even in Japan which was far from the war. The 76th AAA Battalion was transferred from Camp Zama to Showamachi. We were assigned to protect the airfields at Tachikawa and Yokota. Since I had advance notice of the move, I sent Nobi up to Showamachi to find us a place to live before all the others who had girlfriends did the same. Soon after we moved, Nobi told me that she was pregnant and wanted to know what I wanted to do about it. I told her that I loved her very much and that we would keep the baby and that I would support her and the baby no matter what came later in our lives.

The old men of the village sometimes got together. After they got used to me and I believed that they liked me, they would sometimes let me join in while they were drinking. One night while drinking with the men, I got so drunk that I tried to get into the well to get a drink of water. It took all of the menfolk and some of the women to prevent me from drowning myself. I have no idea why I wanted a drink so bad. It was also my luck that this happened on a weekend because I had such a headache that I slept most of the next day. One fine Sunday later in June, Nobi and I were spending the day in Yokohama near the waterfront It was about three or four o'clock in the afternoon when four landing ship transports (LST) pulled into the harbor as we watched. I made the remark that some poor souls were going to be shipped to Korea. These words were not out of my mouth five minutes before the alert sirens sounded which required all military personnel to return to camp. Upon arrival at camp, I learned that it was our unit that was to be shipped to Korea. I only had a few hours to get to Nobi and let her know that I would be going off to war. I assured her that everything would be alright and that all I wanted her to do was to care for our child when it was born and to continue to love me. She then told me that if I happen to get wounded, it would not matter to her if I lost both legs and arms, she wanted me to come back to her. Now that it was well between us, with confidence I was off to Korea and to war.

Chapter 2

KOREAN WAR YEARS

After arriving in Pusan Korea (we could defend only the area around the port of Pusan) I soon learned how to communicate by letter with Nobi and when payday came, I learned how to safely send her money to take care of our home, such as it was. I was lonely for her at first and looked forward to her letters. Even though they were written daily; I received them two or three at a time. Of course I wrote to her each and every day no matter what I had to do. We had a building on the outskirts of the city that appeared to have been a school, so I had space for our company office.

One day I received a letter from her asking if it would be alright if sometimes she went to the club with her girlfriend and her girlfriend's boyfriend. I do not believe her pregnancy had begun to show, so I guess she did fit well in her clothes. I had to admit that I had to search my soul for this request as I am sure I did not want her to go clubbing without me. While I was there with her, we did not go to the club too often. Normally I do my letter writing soon after supper because our lighting was by lanterns, so this night I was very late starting because I was not sure of what I was to write in answer to her request. Of course she explained that she wanted to ask my permission because she was afraid that the word that she was going to clubs would reach me and I would be upset and angry with her. After much thought this is what I said in my return letter:

Dear Sweetheart;

I love you so very much. I think that I have loved you from the time I met you in Zama while we sat talking on the rock. I will get right to your request. I have no intention of ever trying to control you or anything you choose to do. I want you to know that I trust you and know that I believe you will always do right by me, so go and have a good time. I know you like dancing and music and that I do not care much for these things and you have been kind not to insist on going to clubs while I was there with you.

I would like to explain why I did not like going to clubs. First I could not dance well. This was because I was considered smart in school and skipped a grade and I began school when I was five years old because then we could start school in January. By the time I reached high school where the skill of dancing is honed, I did not have much of a social life. Being two grades above my peers the girls would not date someone as young as I. I also worked because my parents could not give me the things that I liked; things like flying lessons, model airplanes, etc.

My beautiful babe was right in her thinking to let me know about her going to the club because soon afterwards someone did write to tell me that they had seen her at the club. I thanked him, but told him that I knew she was going and that in her letters to me she wrote in detail about her adventure there. I heard no more from this individual.

It was not very long afterwards that the command began getting divisions more troops and heavier equipment, bigger tanks and guns. We then broke out of the Pusan perimeter and began to move north. We moved the battalion from Pusan to a town called Taegu. The war was going well for us now and front lines were now into North Korea and there were rumors that we would be moving again.

I had received a letter from my sweetheart that she was not going to the club anymore because she was too big for her clothes and that the baby would be coming soon. I was happy about that even though I trusted her enough to know that she would be true to me whether she went to the club or not. The rumors of us moving grew more intense and sure enough we did get orders to move north to protect the air field at Kempo, just east of Seoul. We also set up positions around Eighth Army Headquarters in Seoul. This was a time when our fighter planes were doing a lot of damage in the north because the enemy air force had all but been destroyed. I mention this because it is the only time we were ordered to shoot down one of our own fighters. It appeared that the pilot thought he was further north than he really was. He saw this large installation on the ground and began to strafe this compound which was Eighth Army Headquarters. Several attempts were made on the radio to make the pilot aware of his error to no avail. Since no one was hurt yet and it was known that his next pass would be with rockets or bombs, we were ordered to bring him down. With our old weapons and the speed of the new jets, our gunners could only hit the tail. This was enough though because the pilot could not control the plane and had to bail out. Through all of this, no one was hurt.

Nothing much happened either with Nobi and me or the war that was worth mentioning except that it was not getting cold. Our company headquarters was located in some houses on the west side of the air base, so we were not exposed to the weather very much. We shared the mess hall with the air force, so we ate well (the air force always had better food because they could fly some from Japan when rations were poor).

It was very late in November, in the year of 1950 when I received a letter from my honey that she had given birth to a baby boy and that he was healthy and weighed around 8 pounds. She also told me that she had named him James Woodfin Washington, Junior. She had also gone to the proper authorities and registered him. There were no cigars to pass out but I strutted around like a peacock and passed out cigarettes.

Soon after I received the news of James' birth, a new program came out called "rest and relaxation", R&R for short. Since we came to Korea as a unit, we all had the same number of points toward R&R, therefore he who put his name in for it, was awarded it sooner. Places where one could go on R&R included Japan, Hawaii, Australia, could stay in the safe part of Korea, Philippians, or anywhere the army had made arrangements for hotel accommodations. Of course I wanted to see my new baby so I immediately put in for Japan. It goes without saying that I was not the only one applying so the list was long. The period of R&R was seven days after you were released from the processing station. What this meant was that the time it took for travelling to your destination, given hot baths, deloused and given clean clothes (they burned your combat clothes), was all duty time.

When you were fully processed your R&R time started, with return time being not later than midnight seven days later. My name finally came to the top of the list and I was sent to Camp Drake, which was some distance north of Tokyo. It seemed like it took forever to get processed as I had a long ways to go to get to Showamachi to see my son. Nobi sent pictures to me with almost every letter. I could see that he was growing and I wanted to be there. Upon being released, I had to first take a bus, then a train and then another train so it was dark when I got there. The house where she lived had the wooden doors in place that covered the paper doors. Normally they stay this way until morning; however the house owner opened them for me. Nobi did not know that I was coming on R&R because I did not have time to write and tell her, so she was very much surprised. In the house where we were staying, there were three or four other young women whose boyfriends were in Korea. The old people who owned the place also acted as chaperones. Would you believe that all of these girls thought our son James was so pretty that they all wanted to hold him in their arms? I do not believe that his feet ever touched the floor. Also these same girls would not leave Nobi and I alone either, even though we were wishing they would go to their own rooms.

When we did get some privacy we tore into each other's arms like there would be no tomorrow. I had been gone for a long time and needed to make love. After making love, we held each other for the rest of the night. Thank God that James did not cry at all so my beautiful babe did not have to get up for him. I had six more days of heaven and I did not want to waste a minute of it. There was not much to do in Showamachi except go to the Base Exchange so I am sure we did that, just the three of us. Everywhere we went, we took James, even to the movies at Tachikawa. I do not remember everything we did on this R&R adventure, but I do remember a lot of hugging and kissing for the entire period. Then my time was up and I had to start back to Camp Drake where my R&R would end. The trip back to Korea would be duty time. After I returned to my unit, which took two or three days I received a letter from her telling me that the day after I left, her period started.

Nobi and I wrote to each other almost on a daily basis but what I enjoyed most was when she sent me a "care" package. The contents of the top part of these "care" packages was two regular little containers of rice crackers and things like that, but under the false bottom, there was seven half pint bottles of Suntory whisky packed in straw to prevent breakage. All of my friends also enjoyed it when my packages came. Sometimes the guys went out in town and bought Korean whisky, but it was terrible tasting and there were rumors that it contained wood alcohol. I do not know how true the rumor was, but I do know that it did taste very bad, so all my friends waited for my "care" packages.

About a month after I returned from R&R we all thought that the war would be over because the North Korean army had been beaten and our troops were standing on the border with Manchuria. Little did we know that ill winds were blowing our way General McArthur wanted to go further but President Truman was afraid that this would turn into a general war, so he called General McArthur to Hawaii and fired him and he was succeeded by General Ridgeway. In any event, the Chinese began to amass an army on their side of the border and when they were ready, poured across the border into North Korea trapping so many of our troops. Some troops were taken off the peninsula by boat while others made their way south over land. It was so hard to stop the Chinese because there were so many of them. We were outnumbered at least five to one.

This is when the great experiment was conducted with our battalion. There was a valley through which the Chinese were sure to come. Here we dug our halftracks into the side of the hill and waited. They came at night blowing horns and making lots of noise. At first it was like shooting fish in a barrel until the antiaircraft guns began to get hot. Antiaircraft weapons are not made for sustained use, but to be shot in short bursts. Since there were so many of them our weapons became ineffective and we had to leave them and run for safety. The next day the infantry had to take back our equipment. It was not long after this that one day while going to breakfast, we noticed that the air force personnel together with all the aircraft were gone. Sometime during the night they packed up and left. The next day some Infantry troops passed through our area whereas we learned that they were the last of the infantry that was north of us. This called us to be on full alert, everyone ready to do combat if necessary. Our commanding officer was calling to group headquarters looking for movement orders to somewhere south. He was told, "If you want movement orders, you had better issue them yourself and get the hell from up there".

Now it was a matter of destroying everything that could be of use to the enemy. All building had to be burned to the ground. Equipment that we could not move had to be blown up. I happen to get on the detail to burn everything which would make me be one of the last to leave the compound. When everything was set, buildings soaked with gasoline and/or napalm, our unit moved out enroute to points south. Together with another corporal, we began our task of igniting the fires so that we also could leave. Soon the entire airbase was burning and we got into our jeep and headed south, so we thought. When we arrived at the main road, it appeared that we should go straight not knowing that the road curved to the north. Sloan was driving as I read the map. We drove along this road until we came to a little town that was on the map. It was at this time that we learned that we were travelling north. We also wondered why we had not caught up with the convoy. During our travel north, we did not encounter another living soul or animals either. We wasted no time turning around and driving very fast. As we passed our old camp, it was still burning. Sloan and I soon caught up with the rest of the unit travelling south.

Our unit finally got settled in our new home, which were tents because all the buildings in the area had been taken. The fighting had begun to seesaw back and forth along the 38th parallel. It was very difficult to gain ground because the Chinese had too many people, so it looked as if we would be in this location for a long time. Nothing much happened for a while, but one morning the first sergeant was found dead. He had just died during the night. Without a first sergeant I had a hard time because all of the senior sergeants were calling me for information. There was not too much I could do, it was up to the company commander to appoint his replacement. Before the day was over, this was settled and the company got back down to business.

One bright and sunny day we received a regulation that would change my life for the better. This regulation authorized marriages between American soldiers and foreign nationals. The requirements were very strict because upon consummating the marriage, the foreign national would be granted non- quota visas to the United States with permanent residency. At this time, visas to Asians were on a very limited quota system, so this non-quota permanent residency status was conducive to fraud. This meant that a soldier could marry a woman for money and when they arrive in America would get a divorce and her non-quota status would still be good. Therefore the marriage application process was designed to prevent fraud. The following is a list of the documents that was contained in the marriage application:

> The applicant must make a request to the Criminal Investigation Department to investigate the background of his intended

bride. An inquiry is made to the local police department for every place she has resided.

The family registry completed in Japanese and must be translated by a bonded translator who is required to sign a statement that it is a true translation of the original document.

Each of us was required to be interviewed by the Chaplain. Some Chaplains were against interracial marriages so it was necessary to get his approval. Because we had a child, it appeared we had an easier time than those without.

Blood test of the intended bride.

A statement attesting that my future bride would not ever seek public assistance such as welfare or even Army Emergency Relief, unless the assistance was in the form of a loan.

The application was very lengthy, three pages long, with almost everything about each of us that they could think of.

This is all of the documents that I could remember, but each level of command must approve the application with final approval given by the Commanding General, Eighth U.S Army. I was surprised that Nobi was able to obtain the documents she was required to get and send them to me by mail. When I put the application together, one copy was almost an inch thick. Of course every piece of correspondence the army sends is in at least triplicate. After I submitted our application, all we could do was to wait. In about a month we finally got our approval. I hate to say this even now that some of the girls that lived nearby were not so lucky and their applications were turn down. About the same time, a new regulation came out outlining the rotation policy since most of us by now had been in Korea for at least eighteen months.

Finally the time for me to rotate from Korea came. My approved marriage application was supposed to have been placed in the record jacket, but I was so afraid that it would be mishandled or lost that I hand carried it myself, only enclosing a copy of the approval in the record jacket. We were given ninety days upon arrival in Japan to complete the marriage and apply for the visa. Just like when I went on R&R, I was sent to Camp Drake. This was a long ways from Showamachi but I did not care, I would gladly make the trip daily since I was officially still on duty with the understanding I could get off when we had appointments.

Chapter 3

MARRIAGES, VISA, AND HOME TO THE STATES

Our first official act was to take the completed and approved marriage application to the American Consulate in Tokyo. There they made sure everything was complete. We were then given an appointment to return for the civil marriage ceremony. If one wanted a religious ceremony, it would have to take place afterwards. In the meantime we were required to publish bans in the local newspapers so that anyone who might have a claim on either of us had a chance to make this known to the consulate.

Hooray! The day for the big event is finally here, January 11, 1952. We got up early and carefully dressed in our best clothes. I had to wear a uniform because civilian clothes were not allowed at this time while overseas. During this period military personnel were required to ride the Japanese trains in specially marked cars. All of the prior mention of taking the train, we rode in cars with the Japanese people because they could not use the specially marked cars. Today, we both rode to Tachikawa in the military personnel cars, and then on to Tokyo on a larger and faster train. As I remember, our appointment was for 11:00 AM at the consulate. We arrived only a few minutes before they were ready for us. I remember I had to hold James because there was no place to sit down and the ceremony consisted mainly on signing papers and answering a few questions, like "do you take this woman for your lawful wedded wife" with the same question to her. We were then married. We received the certificate in two copies and were warned against making other copies. We also made application for the visa to enter the United States.

When we arrived back at Showamachi the first thing I wanted to do was to get her a ring. At a little store near the train station I was able to purchase a simple gold ring as this is all we could afford then. Although later in our lives, I was able to and did purchase her much more expensive rings; she never took off the simple gold ring we bought on the day we were married. Our next step was to go to the nearby Air Force Base to get her an Identification card. We were now an official American family; all military facilities were available to her so we went to the Post Exchange just so she could see what it was like. She only bought cigarettes because it was the only time she could legally have them.

The next day when I went to work at Camp Drake, I reported my marriage. I learned that I would be authorized a housing allowance and since I was on temporary duty, I also would be authorized a per diem allowance of $2.57 per day. Gee, I was going to have much more money than I thought. When I arrived back home to Nobi and told her about the additional money, we agreed that we should save as much as we could because we probably would need it on our trip to the states. After we were married, I noticed that her girlfriends that had been so close to her now seemed to distance themselves although they were still friendly when talking to them. I asked Nobi about this, but I did not receive an answer that meant anything. Being young and naïve, I pushed for a better answer but later I wished that I had not. The real reason was that they knew she was going to the states and most of them would not.

Time passed at its usual pace; I went daily to the camp; Nobi began to integrate American type food into our diet; and James was walking very well now. Nobi, James and I sometimes walked together holding hands sometimes as far as the airbase. Nobi had applied to the Japanese government for a passport, so now we were just waiting for her visa to be approved and her passport to arrive. As always when you are waiting, nothing much happens and time passes slowly. Several weeks passed uneventful but finally she was notified to pick up her passport. A few more weeks later I was notified that her visa had been approved, but we must return to the consulate to have her fingerprints taken again because the first set could not be read. We went and had this done without delay because this was holding up our trip home. Now we were waiting for a call to the port as everything was ready. Our call to the port was on May 8, 1952. We went to the Post Exchange and bought a steamer trunk to pack her clothes along with those for James. My things had to go into my duffel bag because of military regulations. We decided to sell our other things because they could not be used in an American house.

On the morning of May 8 we took off for Yokohama and to the port where our boat was docked. There were many soldiers with dependents waiting to board. Those in my pay grade had previously been made aware that we might not be able to stay with our wives, unless there was room in the part of the boat set aside for dependents. Although I was put into the cabin with Nobi and James, I understood that at any moment they might put another woman there and I would have to go with the troops. About midafternoon, the boat weighed anchor and we began to pull away from the docks. Still I had not been asked to move so I was safe for the entire journey. About a day out to sea, Nobi got seasick and stayed that way until we were pulling into Puget sounds in Washington State. Our ship was of the type we called a round bottom boat which meant it did not displace much water as far as ships go. Also military ships do not have stabilizers to keep the boat from rocking and rolling.

From about 2 days out the sea was rough so only James and I were the only ones who went to all meals in the dining room. Everyone else was in their rooms seasick. All of the waiters knew James because he would beat his entire meal into the plate. He did not eat anything. As a joke, the waiters would come over to our table and ask James what he wished to eat, but immediately said, "It doesn't matter, and you will just beat it into the plate". After a few days I began to worry about Nobi because she had not had anything to eat since the first day at sea and the entire voyage was to take thirteen days. She also would not go to sick bay for something for her seasickness. I even tried to bring food back from the dining room but she just could not eat anything and was vomiting several times per day. I even went and asked the doctor for something for her but he said unless she came in, he could not dispense medicine to me for her. I tried to take her up on deck for fresh air, but when she saw all of that water, she vomited all over me.

There was nothing to do now but hope the voyage would soon be over and eventually it was. As we neared land, the boat rocked and rolled much less and she began to get better. Later that day we docked in Seattle. As we began to disembark I learned some bad news. There was another soldier with the name of James Washington and for some reason he was always ahead of me in the line. Wouldn't you know it, everything done for him and done with my paperwork? I wanted advanced travel pay, he wanted train tickets. I wanted my regular pay, since I had a long ways to go, he didn't want pay, etc. He had my paperwork so messed up, Nobi and I had to be put up in a hotel for the night and go to Fort Lawton the next morning to get everything straight. This did not cost me any leave time, but just inconvenient for us. The officer in charge of personnel felt so sorry for us that he sent us to the train station in an army vehicle. I was happy about that because the only other way was to go by taxi with the cost coming out of my pocket. We boarded a big diesel train that was very fast for that time, bound for Chicago. There we took another train south to Little Rock. By the time we arrived in Little Rock, it was well after dark. We were able to get a taxi to my mother's house. As we were about to knock, I felt Nobi trying to hide behind me. I was not holding her hand because James had fallen asleep and I was carrying him. The taxi driver put our bags on the porch, as I had paid him with tip before we got out of the cab. Mama opened the door and was surprised because we did not tell her we were coming. She went right for James, saying "what a pretty baby, let me hold him." Nobi was still hiding behind me even when I tried to introduce her. Mama finally asked her what was the matter and Nobi said she thought mama was going to hit her. Mama wanted to know why she thought that and Nobi said, "For marrying Bootsie". Mama laughed out loud. My Nobi was alright then. Word soon got out that I was back and a few of the little girls that I had been seeing began to call on the phone. I tried to tell them that I was married now but was not believed until my wife took the phone away from me and told the girl to stop calling her husband or there would be hell to pay. After then I got no more phone calls.

We stayed in Little Rock for 15 days before leaving for Wisconsin as I was to be assigned to Camp McCoy which was between the little towns of Sparta and Tomah.

Chapter 4

OUR FIRST STATESIDE ASSIGNMENT

We thought it best to go to our new place to live with enough time for us to set up our living arrangements. We had no idea what type accommodations we could get or in which of the two little towns, Sparta or Tomah, we would live. When we got there, it appeared that Sparta had more to offer so we decided on settling there. We had to live in the hotel for about five days because we could not find anything to rent and quarters on the post were nonexistent. On our fifth day of looking for a place to live, I could tell my bride was getting restless and wanted to get on with setting up our house. I heard of an old man who had a house for sell so I went to see him and when the conversation was over we were the owners of a nice little house on a side street that was quiet. This is what we were looking for except we wanted to rent, not buy. Since we had no furniture, our next problem was to buy some. Because we had never bought anything on credit, it was very hard to get someone to take the chance on us. We exhausted the new furniture so our only other option was to try the used furniture store. We picked out the things that we wanted, however the owner came up with the same old song and dance about credit. As my niece Cheryl would say, "The Washington in me came to a head", so I said to the man, "Look, we are newlyweds coming from Japan where there were no need for credit, someone has to be the first to give credit to everyone, so it might as well be you". He told me I was right and he delivered our things that day.

It was now time for me to report in for duty. As soon as I started for the camp, it was evident that I had a new problem. The bus that operated between Sparta and the camp would not get me there in time for the morning formation that everyone was required to attend. My memory here becomes vague as I am not sure who I got a ride with as I was never late, but I do not quite remember why I had to stop riding with whom I was riding. Also the upstairs of our little house was not used by us and what caused us to rent it, but in order to go on with my story, I had to buy a car and we had a lodger living at our house. I went to the local used car lot and selected a car, a 1949 mercury four door sedan. I examined the car very well and decided to buy it. We filled out all the paperwork and the bank financing and then took the car for a drive, with the salesman driving. He drove into a service station and filled the tank with gas, then got out and went back to his office. I do not know why I thought we would return as I did not know how to drive. The car had a manual transmission, commonly called a stick shift. I sat there in the service station with cars pulling in behind me. As I started to get behind the wheel and try to move the car, our lodger came walking down the street. I called him over and he was able drive the car home. He also took me and the car out on a little travelled road and began to teach me to drive. Even my wife laughed at how bumpy and jumpy the ride was with me behind the wheel. I soon get to hang of it and the ride became smooth and my gear shifting was without grinding noise. All the while our lodger and his wife was with us, we took the car to the camp together, with him helping with the gas purchase. As I remember, he worked at the airfield and with the cold weather, gas was never kept in the planes overnight, so instead of draining it onto the ground, he drained it into a gas can and we put it into my car. The gasoline used in light planes was just a premium grade and ran very well in my car.

The nice weather of summer soon gave way to fall with chills in the air. The city put out an ordinance requiring all home owners that were not using all of the land on their property and such unused property that had overgrown with weeds must have the weeds cut by the end of November. The neighbor on my right side was an old grouchy man who immediately thought to solve the problem by setting his weeds on fire. When the fire trucks came and put the fire out, he was given a stern warning not to try that again. The neighbor on my left came home one evening with a horse drawn scythe. I came out to watch because I had never seen such an instrument. When he had finished, I asked him if I could borrow that thing and he agreed to let me use it. When he handed me the reins guiding the horses, he knew right away I did not know anything about horses, so he told me to get out of the way and he mowed mine too.

I do not know how I could have overlooked it, but I woke up one Thursday morning and realized that it was Thanksgiving, the first in our new home. Somehow I had forgotten to buy even a chicken for this day. There were other things in the house like vegetables and rolls, but no bird. All the stores were closed and I was sunk. I could not blame Nobi because Thanksgiving is an American holiday therefore she could not know what day it was celebrated. It was entirely my fault. I went out to see if there was something I could remotely use for a Thanksgiving dinner but there were hardly anyone on the streets and no stores open. I met a teen aged boy with a large fish. I asked him to sell it to me and that I would give him five dollars for it. He wanted ten dollars and we settled on seven dollars and fifty cents. Our first Thanksgiving dinner consisted of the fish, vegetables, rolls and lemonade. I promised myself that I would not slip up on Christmas. I need not have worried because Nobi knew all about Christmas and all I had to worry about were getting a Christmas tree.

It was now in the middle of December when one day we were driving home from work, it had snowed and snow was still coming down. Another car was following me about two minutes behind. The highway had light traffic I guess because of the snow. There was a turn in the road where I pulled straight off the roadway to discharge a passenger who was now riding with us. As we were saying our "goodbyes", the car that was following us was using my tracks as a guide but realized too late that I had pulled straight off the roadway at the turn, so he tried to swerve back onto the road and skidded right into a telephone pole. My lodger, the passenger I had just discharged from my car and I went over to the accident and determined that no one was injured and not too much damage to the car, we left to come home. Because mostly military personnel use this section of the highway, the military police patrolled it with the county's blessing. About an hour after getting home I was paid a visit by the military police asking me why I left the scene of an accident. I told him it was because I was not involved because we had been sitting still, off the road for about two minutes before the other car hit the telephone pole. This satisfied him and he told me that my explanation was supported by the facts found at the scene. He further told me that he also thought that the people in the other car were trying to remove blame from them.

What happened next was the lowest point in my long life with Nobi, whom I have love with all my heart from the beginning. I hope those who read this will not judge me too harsh, not because I deserved it, but because the outcome brought us so much closer together. Our lodger had found larger quarters for himself and his wife, so only Nobi, James and I lived in our little house. We had the steamer trunk that we had bought from the Base Exchange before leaving Japan. It placed near the door and was being used as a chest of drawers since one side of it had drawers. I do not know why I looked into the steamer trunk because I was not looking for anything. There I found a letter addressed to some of her friends that were still in Japan. I took the letter into the attic, opened and read the letter, since it was written in English. She was asking them to send her money if they could. She also said to them that I was so young and naïve. I was so hurt from reading this I sat down to wonder what brought this on. I thought we were doing great. I knew we were not rich, but our bills were always paid on time, we had enough to eat daily and we had sufficient clothing. My hurt began to turn to anger, so I came down with fire in my eyes and ask her, "What is this" and before she could answer I slapped her so hard with my open hand that she fell over onto the couch. I was going to hit her again, but I caught myself, bit my tongue, and sat down. I then asked her again, "What is this". Here I got the surprise of my life. This is what she told me, "You are in a dangerous profession. If anything ever happens to you, what am I to do? I do not know anyone here and nobody to help me". I tried to tell her all the things she would be entitled to if I died while on active duty or was killed. She answered, "This is all well and good, but for me to get the money will take time and I will need money to restart my life". I felt so ashamed of myself but I did say to her that we should tell each other our fears and not try to act on them alone, and that we should always talk to each other and never to go to bed angry at each other.

I know lots of couples say these things, but we always did from this day. I made a vow to myself that I would never, never strike her again. I can safely say that from that day on, I never did. This was not the end because now her fears were now my problem. I knew that she had a legitimate fear of being left alone in a strange place with a child and with no one who really cared for her. She really did need some money she could have immediate access to, enough so that if decided, she could return to Japan where people knew her. I knew that it would be hard for me to save such a sum on my pay and expenses and that my wife, whom I loved with all of my heart, was really afraid and could not stand it for long. I could not let her become depressed. My enlistment was near, so I took a short discharge and reenlisted for six more years. I grossed about fifteen hundred dollars from this exchange. I took one thousands of these dollars and put into a savings account because I was not too worried about interest payments, but for immediate access. I brought the bank book home and gave it to her and told her it was for her to keep wherever she wanted and hoped that she would now feel safe. Her face beamed and glowed like it did when we first met sitting on the rock. I think for the first time she was sure that I could solve problems and that I really could take care of her. I did not see that little bank book for many of years. As I said earlier, we were drawn much closer after this. She was sure that even though I was young, I was a man. We began to talk to each other about the things that cause couples to divorce. One of the main reason being the use of, or the lack of money. We agreed that any money that came into our house, regardless of who earned it; each would have equal say about the use thereof. The other reason couples get divorced is infidelity. We vowed to be true to each other and to trust each other even with our lives. I am sure that on this day we removed the biggest stumbling blocks from our young lives.

Winter gave way to spring and it began to warm up, so James could now play outside. One Saturday while he was playing outside by himself, he decided he would go downtown and explore. He had been gone about a half hour before Nobi missed him. She looked around the house both inside and out but could not find him. Sparta was a little town so the downtown area began about three blocks away, but James had to turn the corner on the main street to get there. Of course we were frantic and immediately began looking for him, first closer to home and then widening our search. When we got to the downtown area, we went into each store, bar, hotel asking if they had seen a little boy wander through. We soon began to get word that he had passed through about 15 minutes ago or so. Others in the town began to help us find James and soon almost everyone in the downtown area was helping us look. When we found him, he was on his way back home.

We were so glad to get him back that he did not get a spanking, just hugs. James could not understand what all the fuss was about and told us so. We explained to him why he should not wander off by himself as harm could come to him.

Soon after we lost James, I came home from work to find my sweetheart of a wife looking very sad, although things in the house seemed normal and I could not see anything to make her sad. She then told me that she was pregnant, although we had been trying to delay having another child until we had more money. I held my darling in my arms and told her not to worry; we would love this child just as much as we loved the one we had. As I continued to hold her, I said to her, "Honey, don't be sad about this child, God must have wanted us to have it, so let us be happy about it". She wondered whether we would have enough money to buy the things necessary for a new baby. I told her we had plenty of time to prepare if we started now, so we began to save any and every small amount left over at the end of the month when we were paid again.

Time passed as we scrimped and saved for our new baby. Then we received a blow to our plans and progress. Camp McCoy was going to close and the 68th Engineer Group and its three battalions would be transferred to Camp Carson, Colorado. By now Nobi was seven months pregnant and by army rules and regulations was not permitted to travel. The personnel of my unit moved while we were left behind waiting for our baby to be born. A month passed, Nobi was now eight months. We were shocked when we were told that the hospital was going to close and that I had better go out to Colorado. It was too late to sell our house, pack and ship our things, so the best we could do was to sell our furniture back to the second hand dealer and ask the man who sold us the house to take it back. It was alright with him because he never transferred the house to us with the county. I am sure that that old man had sold that house to soldiers more than once. The next day we packed our clothes and packed the car with everything we could carry and departed for our new home in Colorado.

Chapter 5

MOVING TO COLORADO

We started driving along highway 16 going west on into Minnesota. The first night we got a little past a town called Albert Lea when it became late so we began to look for lodging for the night. We stayed at a little motel that was not too expensive. Upon arising the next morning we discovered that during the night came a blizzard. All the ground and streets were covered with what looked like one continuous sheet of ice. While I could drive pretty fair now, I was not prepared for driving in this type of weather; however we were under pressure to get to Colorado before the baby was born. I collected my thoughts about snow and ice driving, remembering that if I began to skid, to turn into the skid. Cautiously we proceeded to continue on our journey down the highway. I was driving very carefully and was doing great until I had to drive down a small hill. I could see no danger because I had driven down such a hill even on this journey so I proceeded. About half way down, I began to skid. I turned into the skid like the driving manual said, but nothing happened, the car kept going across the roadway and onto the shoulder on the wrong side of the road. My car still did not stop, but came to rest with the front wheels hanging over an embankment. God must have been with us because when I got out of the car to access the damage, the snow plough was right there and the operator just hooked onto my car and pulled it out and placed it on the right side of the road. We then cautiously continued on our journey thinking of how lucky we were.

When we got almost through the state of Minnesota, we passed under a bridge and then the highway markings indicated that we were in South Dakota. I knew that this was wrong because I knew my next state would be Iowa. We backtracked until the highway markings indicated we were on the right trail and turned around and proceeded carefully. There was no highway marking to say otherwise, so I passed again under the same bridge only to get the same results. I did this about three times before I realized that maybe I was supposed to turn and go over the bridge. There I found the right roadway so we proceeded on. That day we crossed from Iowa into Kansas before we had to stop. We stopped for our evening meal at a little restaurant. We decided to splurge and each ordered a steak dinner thinking we would get regular portions. When the food came, one plate would feel all three of us. The lady there was nice and packed the meal that we did not eat so that we could have it the next day. The ice and sleet was all gone now so we could make better time. We shot across Kansas into Colorado along highway 50 which would take us into Colorado Springs. We had to stop one more time after crossing the Kansas/Colorado border because we wanted to arrive in the day. We knew we would have to find some kind of lodging so arriving in the daytime was paramount.

 The first thing we did was to buy a newspaper and look at ads for apartments and/or rooms for rent. We tried apartments first since we are going to need room for the three of us and later for the new baby. I guess that since the whole group (headquarters and three battalions) were there, there were no more apartments to rent. We went looking for room rentals as a temporary measure. The next two ads we answered, I went to make the rental and was immediately told, "We rented the rooms just before you came". After the second rejection, I began to feel that the "ugly face of prejudice" was at play here, as I was under the impression that Colorado did not have such a thing. The next ad on our list, I sent Nobi to make the rental and James and I stayed in the car which was out of sight. Sure enough she made the rental but when the woman saw us, she knew she had been tricked. She could not retract the agreement because we would have had a case. Because I knew that we had tricked the landlord, we would not be happy there, nor would the woman want us to stay so we immediately started looking for lodging. While at work a few days later, we were discussing living arrangements, the personnel sergeant, whose name was Bash, told me that the camp had some barracks that had been converted into family quarters and they only cost between one half and two thirds of our quarters allowance. He also told me that the apartment right across the hall from him was vacant. I immediately got into my car and drove, rather swiftly, to the post billeting office to see if I could obtain one of these quarters. Luck again was with me because I was able to get the set of quarter's right across the hall from my personnel sergeant with whom I worked. It did not take us long to move since we only had our clothes. In addition, we could get furniture without additional cost. This would give Nobi and me lots of time to buy our own furniture if so chose.

On the night of January 31, 1953 it was time for Nobi to go to the hospital for the purpose of delivering our baby. She labored through the night so on the morning of February 1, 1953 our daughter made her debut into the world. Sergeant Bash, who lived across the hall from us, was married to a German woman. We were in a fog as what to name our new daughter when I remembered Mrs. Bash saying that if she ever had another daughter, she would name her "Eva Maria". I asked her if I could use that name because I thought it was a lovely name. Mrs. Bash said she was not planning on any more children and it was perfectly alright for me to use the name. When I went to the hospital that day, I told Nobi about the name and that it came from Mrs. Bash. Nobi also liked the name so we told the hospital that we had named our daughter "Eva Maria".

Time passed with nothing much happening. I had changed the car from the 1949 Mercury to a 1951 Hudson and had gone to Denver with Sergeant Bash to help him pick out a used car for himself because he did not own a car at this time. A little later promotion came out and I was promoted to Sergeant and Bash to Sergeant First Class. This meant a little more money and a larger quarters allowance without an increase in the cost of our quarters.

As I write this, even to myself, it appears that I am the one who are making all of the decisions. That is not the case. If there was a decision to make, we made it together. We paid our bills together and made purchases together. Nobi was not only my wife and lover, she was my partner and I would not ever think of deciding anything without consulting her. We had complete trust in each other as well as confidence in each other's ability.

It is now winter and we had been invited to some friend's house for dinner. While there it snowed very hard and snow covered everything. When we were ready to go home I drove onto what I thought was the street and went right into a ditch. It is a good thing that the ditch was not too deep and I was able to put the car in reverse and slowly backing out. I got out of the car and manually searched for the street. My beautiful and dear wife laughed at me, and laughed all the way home.

I know that there were more happenings other than going to and from the camp on a daily basis, but I am not able to remember anything unusual going on between the winter and the next spring when the next event occurred. I do not even remember Christmas this year. I am sure that the children received an allotment of toys and games. I knew there was something; this is the year that I bought for my babe a fur coat. I had to order it through the Sears.

Catalog and have it delivered at Sergeant Bash's residence so she would not see it before Christmas. My Honey would not wear this coat and would not tell my why, at least not now. I did find out why she would not wear it and learned something about my wife that I did not know. While I did not pay a fortune for the coat, if she had told me sooner, I could have returned it for something she would use. The reason turned out to be that some animals had to be killed to make the coat and she could not stand the thought of this. Nobi had such a kind heart, especially for animals that if we were driving through the countryside and if it happens to be raining or cold, she would want the farmer to round up the cattle and put them in the barn. I often tried to tell her that God provided for the cattle and that they were alright just as they were. Because we had similar conversations throughout our life together, I do think she bought my explanation.

In the early spring of the next year I received orders to go overseas to Germany. This meant that I would have to travel alone for at least a year before Nobi and the children could accompany me. This was the first time in our married life that I had to leave her. I did not feel good about this but could do nothing about it. She understood that I had to go where the army sent me. Our only choice was either find an apartment in the vicinity of Colorado Springs or I could take her to my parents' home in Little Rock, Arkansas. She chose Little Rock because at least she would be near family members. In addition, we could save a little money not having to pay rent.

Chapter 6

GOING TO GERMANY

After spending my leave time with her and the kids, I was off to Fort Dix, New Jersey where I was processed and boarded a boat to Bremerhaven Germany. We then took another train to Kaiserslautern and after a few days there I received an assignment to Bad Kreuznach. Here I would serve for the next three years. At first I was lonely for my wife and kids but kept busy working. We wrote to each other every day. When we are apart, this we avowed to write something daily. If we were too busy, just "I Love you" was written on the paper and mailed, but she always had something to tell me.

I had not gone for more than a few months when her letters began to have tones of discontent so I asked her why and was told that my parents' house was too crowded in that my sister was undergoing a divorce and had come to live there too. This occurred after I left. I have to admit that I was not prepared for this financially; however I had to do something for my babe and my children. After looking around and asking questions of what others in my situation were doing, I came up with a plan. I told her that she could come to Germany, however until our name came to the top of the housing roster, we had to live as Germans. This would mean that we could not use the commissary nor would the army give us any assistance such as furniture or household goods. We could, however, use the Post Exchange. Any lodging we rented would have to be furnished. She could only bring what she could carry because shipping of household goods would be postponed until we received government quarters. This was fine with her so we began to execute the plan. James was included in her passport and would have to be removed so she had to apply to the Japanese Consulate for a new passport. She also had to go to the Post Office in Little Rock and apply for a passport for both James and Eva. In the meantime, apply to Immigration and Naturalization Service for an Exit/Entry permit. All of this would be required before booking passage on a steamship bound for Germany. Needless to say this took quite sometimes but she was more content with living with the overcrowded conditions with my parents. When all these things were completed, she booked passage on a Dutch ship that was bound for Rotterdam, so I had to meet her there. The American Express was very helpful in booking her passage and making sure that things went according to plan. When I received the information as to her arrival in Europe, I began to look for and rent a place for us to live. Living in the barracks was alright for me but sometimes, especially holidays, I got awful lonesome, and so I wanted my family there as much as she wanted to come. Of course this took a lot of our money, but it was well worth it. The only place I could find in Bad Kreuznach was with some people who operated something like a tavern. The sold mostly wine and made it on the premise.

    The big day finally arrived when Nobi and the children would be arriving at Rotterdam in The Netherlands. I took a few days leave and went by train that travelled overnight to get there. The American Express had made arrangements for us to spend the night there before boarding a train back to Bad Kreuznach. Was I ever glad to see them!

    When we arrived at Bad Kreuznach and proceeded to the place I had rented, I could tell by the frown on her face that all was not well with our living arrangements. Still she did not complain, however I was compelled to explain that this was the only place I could find that had enough room for us. There was a German store right across the street so we did have adequate and shelter. Sometimes at night, I went down in the basement with the owner when he was checking on the wine. It was necessary to taste the wine so he and I both had a glass. Nobi, on the other hand was still not too happy here so I began to look for another place. I soon found another place in Bad Munster about four or five miles away from Bad Kreuznach. In order to get to work on time from here, I must catch the bus at seven o'clock sharp. These buses were never late so I had to be ready and waiting when the bus arrived. I was also able to arrive at the Bad Kreuznach railroad station just in time to catch the army bus for a ride on to work. We lived with a woman named "Anna" in a house very near one that had been bombed out. Nobi was happier here but we had less space. One of the things I remember while living with Anna was the cooking arrangement. Anna had a small tub which she filled with potatoes and boiled then. From this tub she was able to make all meals of the day for her family. Of course Nobi and I made our meals like the Americans that we were. One Saturday I was making a cake for the children and Anna was also making a cake. I made my cake from a "Duncan Himes" box added milk and eggs and had it baked while Anna was still beating and mixing hers. When mine was fully frosted with chocolate from another can, Anna could not understand how a cake could be made in such a short time and be as smooth and delicious as the one I made while she took so much time mixing and beating and hers still came out with the consistency of corn bread.

Up until now, I had not formally celebrated my dear wife's birthday or our anniversary. I am sure I thought enough of her to celebrate it so I conclude that I must not have been present of did not have money when these days occurred. This year I had one of my friends who had commissary privileges to get me two lobster tails. My friend gave them to me immediately upon departing the commissary as I waited outside while he bought them. I took them home and began to prepare them so I am sure they were alright as they were still moderately frozen. I made her a nice birthday/anniversary dinner and after we had eaten, we began to vomit and could not stop. I had to take us both to the hospital emergency while Anna stayed with the children. I am glad the children did not eat any.

Our name finally came to the top of the housing. I was called to the billeting office and was assigned quarters on the fourth floor of a building right across the street from the commissary. Because I was a member of the post, I received the best of the available quarters. I also had first choice. Our new house was equipped with nice furniture, china and glassware, and silverware. Because we had two children being of opposite sexes, our quarters had three bedrooms, living and dining room and a very nice bathroom. Since being married, this was the nicest placed we have lived. The building was placed in a square creating a large playground behind each building. The children were safe there. The only problem was that our children were small and had to go up and down eight flights of stairs in order to reach the playground. Nobi seemed to be happy here and she could have a maid to help her with the children. The maid that we had first came with the house, so we decided to keep her, not knowing anyone else to hire. She also seemed nice and friendly and eager to serve us. On Saturdays after breakfast I took the children down to the playground and played with them along with larger children. One particular Saturday while playing ball with the larger children I was asked if I could hit a baseball over the building. I said that I did not know, so one little child pitched the ball and I hit it high and hard, right into a window on the fourth floor (not mine). The children all ran but I had to set a good example and could not run away. I went up to the apartment whose window I had broken and offered to call and have it fixed after helping to place cardboard over the window until Monday morning. As it turned out, it was a blessing that the ball that I hit broke the window and not continued over the building because there were several cars parked in front of the building and my ball may have done much more damage.

One day we were surprised by a visit from Anna, whose house we had previously lived in before getting American quarters. Nobi showed her the house. Anna seemed pleased that we were having good fortune. Anna had never drunk American type coffee or any of the food she was served at our apartment. When she left to go home, she promised to come and visit often.

As with all good things, there is some bad. A new sergeant who was senior to all who lived in our building was assigned. He had a small son, a little older and bigger than James. This boy was either a bully or he was trying to imitate his father by trying to give orders on the playground. One day while playing in the sandbox he pushed Eva down and James hit him in the eye. He ran home and told his mother. That night his father and mother came up to our apartment in a huff demanding that we punish James for blacking his son's eye. I called James and asked him why he hit him and was told that the other boy had pushed Eva down. I said that I could not punish my son for protecting his sister. The sergeant and his wife again left in a huff vowing to get even. He thought that any little thing that our children did, he tried to report. He did not know that I worked for the Post Adjutant (Chief Administrative Officer) and that my word would supersede his. I also learned that he was not too fond of Sergeant Wilson who also lived on the fourth floor but on the other end of the building with different stairwell. We were both black so we began to think that he did not like black people or as we termed, wanted his building to be lily white.

To get rid of us, he tried to get our wives sent home. He made his maid sign a statement that we spent a lot of time in the maid's quarters in the basement. At this time I am not sure I knew where the maids lived. I think that he knew nothing would come of his complaints if he reported us to the billeting office or to the command, so he went to the CID (Criminal Investigation Detachment) and made his complaint there, armed with his untrue statement from his maid. Wilson and I were called to the CID and asked to make a statement, but slyly advised us not to. Of course this came directly to the Post Adjutant who only teased me about it, and had a big laugh. After that Wilson and I became good friends and often visited each other's apartment. His wife was named Maxine but we all called her Mac.

The Wilsons had a set of twins, a boy and a girl. Their names were Bill Wayne and Betty Lane. One day Nobi and I went over to visit with the Wilsons the twins were studying long division. They were smart kids because Mac made them study and do their homework without fail. Because they were smart kids, I thought I would tell them wrong on their division, but would tell them better before we went home. I told them to do like the following: Subtract the two numbers and that is the answer, i.e. Seven will go into 12 five times, because seven and five are twelve. This sounded like what the teacher told them. The trouble was I forget to tell them better before I went home and they did their whole homework this way. When they got home from school with their whole assignment done wrong, they told their mother that Mr. Washington told us to do our assignment that way. Mac called me up and said, "I'm going to kill you".

Getting acquainted with the Wilsons was very good for us, as we had lots of fun. One night they came to visit us. We played lots of music, danced and drank whisky. As we sat around listing to the music and drinking, Nobi, who could not drink much, got a little too much. She went to the bathroom and after a while when she did not come back, we went to look for her being cautious not to disturb her if she was using the bathroom properly. We found her in the bath tub fully dressed and drunk as a skunk and laughing up a storm. This is the very first time and probably the last time I ever saw my baby drunk. When the Wilsons went back to their apartment, I put her to bed. She had a hangover the next morning so bad that I bet she never forgot it.

There was an open area on the hill behind the hospital that the army had obtained from the Germans. Once per month, as a training exercise, we went into this area to play soldier. The company was divided in half with one group being the attacking force, the other defending. On one occasion, I happen to be on the attacking force and being a sergeant, had the rocket launcher. When I was issued the ammunition, I admit I did not look at it too closely and did not realize that I had a real live phosphorous grenade. As we attacked there were some troops hiding behind some bushes. This would be a good time to fire my grenade. When I fired it, fire went everywhere. We were really lucky because none of the white burning powder got on anyone as it would burn through the skin. It did, however set the bushes and everything around on fire. We all had to stop and put out the fire which took more than an hour. We all then went to our tents and went to bed. The next morning we left the hill and those of us who lived in the housing area were given permission to leave the bus and go home to clean our weapons. We all had learned that to really clean our rifles after shooting blanks, to wash the metal parts with very hot water in the bath tub. This did not go over well with my honey, because she was afraid of guns, did not want them around her children, and she thought washing a gun in the tub would make rings. Nothing I could say to persuade her that it was safe, so I had to walk down the hill and into the company area to clean my gun. I never brought another gun into our house.

Nobi was such a beautiful girl and loved to dance. The few times that we went to the club, several of the men wanted to dance with her and because I always trusted her I did not mind. I could dance the slow dances and I took most of these. I also knew that when it was time to go home, I would be the one she went home with. Sometimes I would just sit and look at her and wonder what I did to deserve this person who is my wife. As I said when we first met that I believed that God gave her to me and I thank Him every day.

The year progresses and now it's into February 1954 and my darling wife informs me once again that she is pregnant. I guess that I should have known this because at times like this, she begins to glow all over and her skin had been glowing for weeks. Of course we had to slow down on our night life, so we went to the Wilsons to celebrate. While we were out, the maid had wanted to wear Nobi's fur jacket. The maid knew that Nobi did not wear the jacket, but did not know why she did not want it, I am sure she kept it because I bought it for her. I am sure this is when the main slipped it out of the closet and down to her room. She should have been looking after the children. When we got home, we got ready for bed and did not even think about a jacket that Nobi would not wear. Sometimes afterwards, while looking for some other garment in her closet, my babe noticed that her fur jacket was stretched out of shape and the fur worn in places. She got so angry with the maid that she told me that I had to fire her immediately. As the maid was leaving, Nobi said to her, "if you had asked me for that jacket, I would have given it to you because I will not wear fur". The maid looked so sick then that I almost felt sorry for her. The next day we put in a request at Civilian Personnel office for another maid and were assigned a girl by the name of Elizabeth, who was much better with the children. As we settled down time passed slowly. I took Nobi to the hospital for her regular checkups with the gynecologist who was taking care of her, as scheduled. The baby was progressing well with complications and then on November 24, Robert Charles Washington came into the world. During this time, husbands and his friends had to wait in the waiting room and were not allowed in the delivery room. It was only after he was cleaned up and given to Nobi that I had a chance to see him. The next morning when I happily announced the birth of my son, the Post Commander asked me, "You have this baby upstairs or downstairs". He was teasing me because of the time when the Sergeant in charge of the house tried to get my wife and Wilson's wife sent home.

Our children began to grow and we doted on our new baby. We continued our friendship with the Wilsons, either going to their house or they coming to ours. When we visited, we had the habit of going down the stairs all the way to the basement; then along to the hallway to the Wilson's stairwell before climbing their stairwell to the fourth floor. When Robert was about two years old, he had made this trip many times with us. One day, while Nobi was busy and not watching him too closely, he made the trip to the Wilsons door, knocked and when Mac opened the door, he looked up at her and said, "Dum Dum" (He was trying to say the German way for Dummy), turned around and came home the same way. Mac called Nobi on the phone and told her that her son had come and called her a dummy, and then they both died laughing. When Mac saw Robert again, she told him if he called her a dummy again, she would get him. This must not have fazed Robert because he did it at least two more times. We could never understand why he wanted to call her that, although it was rather cute and fun, we often wondered if he knew what he was saying.

At work, I had begun to get more responsibility. A new headquarters building had been constructed in the compound where other American facilities were located and returned our old headquarters back to the German government. Also the command took over greater responsibility, so my section grew from a two man unit to six with the addition of the personnel Officer. It is also the time for us to begin thinking about coming back home. This meant going to the American Consulate at Frankfurt to renew Nobi's exit/entry permit, put Robert on the passport issued to James and Eva. Of course this meant making several trips to the consulate, but things went pretty well and by the time I issued my orders to go to Fort Ord, California and received a port call for all of us, we were ready to go. Our departure was to be from Frankfurt Main Air Base because we were to go by air. This pleased Nobi a great deal because she gets seasick easily. When we boarded the plane, we had a little more room because each of the children had their own seat which they did not use but chose to stand by the window and watch the water. We had a stopover at Prestwich Scotland for a few hours and then on to McGuire Air Force Base, New Jersey. Processing through Fort Dix did not take too long and it was still morning when we were released on our own. Our first act was to go to New York and purchase a car because we needed one and our travel would be cheaper. We bought a 1956 Plymouth Belvedere with the push button transmission. As we travelled west and south enroute to Little Rock to see my parents every radio station was playing Doris Day singing "Que Sera, Sera". By the time we got to Pittsburgh we were tired of that song. We pushed on and spent the night in a little place in West Virginia. Here we had a tiny problem with motels and was pushed toward the black section of town. During this time all interstate travel facilities were supposed to be integrated. By the next night we were in Little Rock where we stayed visiting until it was time to head west again to make our home on the west coast. I needed to get some money and from Little Rock, the nearest military installation was at Pine Bluff. When I went there I learned that when I had gone to the finance office in Germany where I knew most everyone working there, and when I was teasing because I was going home and they were staying, after being paid my travel, absentminded I folded up my pay card so the money I drew there was not posted. Now at Pine Bluff,

I could get much more money that I had thought. I told them to just give me the one month's pay and I would straighten everything when I got to Fort Ord. Little did I know that this could not be straightened out and I had to withdraw the money, which I put in the bank as I was sure that the Government would want the money back? To this day the money is still in the bank.

We then departed Little Rock with about twenty days left on my leave because we did not know what obstacle would confront us in setting up our household. We wanted to have ample time so that when I had to report in at Fort Ord, our house would be already for us. James was beginning to go to school and we did not know about this either. It took us about four days to get there. As we passed through the desert area, gasoline prices began to raise, just think they wanted forty three cents for a gallon. We thought this was outrageous, and vowed not to pay it. We almost ran out of gas trying to get close to the coast where gasoline prices returned to twenty-nine or thirty cents.

Chapter 7

OUR STAY AT FORT ORD

We arrived at Fort Ord during the middle of the day and were assigned rooms at the post guest house. It is permissible to remain in the guest house for a maximum of seven days. Little did I know that my stay here would be over the next eight years? Our first try was to the post billeting office for assignment of quarters on the post. There were several types of quarters on the post, however if you wanted standard quarters, your name would be placed on a very long list. You would then have to wait until your name came to the top of the list. There were available converted barracks in an area called Ord Village, similar to those we had in Camp Carson Colorado; where financially you did not forfeit your quarter's allowance, but was charged rent that was payable monthly, normally becoming due on the end of the month. We were assigned Quarters 8C Fremont Circle where my wife became acquainted with another Japanese woman, whose name was Yoshie Carter, who lived across the street. The Carters had two sons who were about the same age as James and Robert. Our friendship with the Carter family lasted until this date and Yoshie became one of Nobi's closest friends.

    Next door to our apartment was a family, whose name I cannot recall at this time (it has been more than 50 years ago) who had a little boy Robert's age. There was a big open space behind the house that extended all the way to California Highway 1. The boys were allowed to play in this area because there was a fence separating this space from the highway, so the boys would not be in danger from it. Robert and this little boy would go and sit by the fence and watch cars passing and count Volkswagens, and call then "putt, putt".

It was not legal to park on the streets in the housing area where we lived. There was a big open space behind our house, so I parked my car there. One evening after returning from work, I parked as usual and went into the house. I did not notice that Robert and the little boy next door went into the car and played with the controls. We had the Plymouth model that had push button gear shifts. I am sure that I put the car in park and the hand brakes on before I left the car. I guess the boys had their fill of pushing the buttons and left the vehicle. The next thing I knew, my car was rolling down the hill, picking up speed as it went. The man next door said that he saw it start rolling, but thought it was a short cut to the highway. I must have been lucky because my car hit a fence around a gas main and stopped. My car was damaged, but was covered by my insurance. The fence around the gas main was also damaged and was covered by my insurance. Robert did not get a spanking.

Christmas of this year was the when bicycles became a part of the Washington's household as James was now big enough to own one and had so requested since other children had them. We went to Sears because that is where we had always had charge accounts and purchased a full sized bike for James, a smaller type bicycle for Eva and tricycle for Robert. As I remember, Robert had to have a cowboy outfit with matching repeater cap pistols, because that was what the boy next door was getting. I had to stay up very late at night assembling two bicycles, and a tricycle. My honey of a wife, although not too much help with the bikes, stayed up with me. On Christmas James and I had our first continuing disagreement over food. Until now, I had not noticed that he was a finicky eater but I guess my wife knew as she is with them more. Breakfast containing eggs were served this Christmas morning but James would not eat his. I told him that he could not leave the table until he did. This included riding his new bike. James sat at the table with the eggs, now cold, all day; neither of us would back down. I just could not understand his reasoning until years later. Needless to say, when it was late in the evening, I said nothing when Nobi gave him something else to eat before going to bed. I was just as glad to see the end of this ordeal. During prior Christmas our children were little and not too much attention had to be paid when purchasing their toys and things. This was also the first year that Nobi and I discussed what to get for them and agreed that the children would get everything that they needed and some of the things they wanted, according to what we could afford. This was our policy during the entire time of their childhood through high school, or until they were old enough to buy it for themselves.

Things in California seemed to be higher than we were used to therefore money was a little tighter. General Mills think that they invented Hamburger Helper, but we were eating it along with other variations of this meal long before one could buy it in a box from the grocery store. My honey got very good at making it and to tell the truth, our whole family enjoyed it. No one ever complained when it was being served for the evening meal.

Our neighbor and Nobi's friend had a husband who drank a lot and sometimes was in trouble with his commander. He was always given some type punishment, including reduction in rank thereby leaving less money for the family. Carter would want to go out in the evenings, but Yoshie did not want him to do so and would get somewhat angry with him. One day she asked me if I would go out with him and try not to let him drink to excess because he could not stand another delinquency report. I agreed to accompany him, so we left home and went out. We arrived at a line of bars along Fremont Street in Seaside, CA and went into the second bar omitting the first in the line. There Carter, who knew most of the drinkers, greeted each as we passed through. Carter did not stop walking, except to have a few words with the ones he was friendlier with. By the time he got to the end door of the bar, which was not very big, he appeared to be drunk, stumbling over his own feet. I know for sure that he did not take a drink of anything much less anything with alcohol in it. Luck was not with him because as soon as he went out of the door, the Military Police was there. I tried my best to explain to them that he could not be drunk because he only walked through the bar without having a drink. My attempt to make them understand was in vain because they wrote him a delinquency report, which was delivered to his commander the next day through the Provost Marshal. Because I knew that Carter had not taken a drink that night, I went to his commander in an attempt to explain exactly what happened and that Carter was sicker than one requiring punishment. While his commander said that he understood, he was required to give him punishment and a report made to the Provost Marshal as to what punishment was given. To this day I believe that Carter had become an alcoholic and the mere breathing of fumes from the whisky in the bars made him drunk. This being the case, Carter should have been designated as being sick but there were no such designation in the army at that time and Carter did not get a fair deal.

During this time Nobi and I found time to be with our children and to take them places. We took them to "Dennis the Menace" playground in Monterey; Santa's Village up on Highway 17 north of Santa Cruz and to the Board Walk in Santa Cruz. James liked to go on a ride called "Wild Mouse" while we took the others on the motor cars. James was limited to three rides because we could not afford to spend too much on these outings. One thing about our children, they never made a fuss when they were told then "No, we can't afford it".

It was popular at this time to make motion pictures of our visits to these places so we too made these movies, mostly of our children to record their progress in growing up. I also tried to get our children interested in airplanes by building models. On one occasion the boys and I built a motor driven control line model that we flew in the area behind our quarters. We had fun with this aircraft until we cracked it up. Seems as though I had more fun than the boys because we did not build another. The boys seemed less interested, so I packed away the engine hoping that one day we would build another. My wife said that I was trying to relive a part of my life by trying too hard to impose my interest upon them. In my youth I had learned to fly real airplanes. I took my lessons from one of the black pilots that flew fighter planes during World War II.

The Army began to build new quarters for both officers and enlisted men in a new area on Fort Ord. When a sufficient number had been completed, personnel living in the standard quarters were required to move into the new quarters, leaving the then standard quarters to those of us whose name had not came to the top of the list. After all of the quarters in an area were vacant, we in Ord Village were given these quarters under the same financial arrangement. We were assigned quarters at 388 Leinbach Avenue, which was in an area called Bay View Park. We were assigned quarters with four bedrooms because our family consisted of two boys and a girl. This was near to the school and better for our children. It was here that the neighborhood children all congregated in our yard. It was mostly because of our children, but also that I came out and played with them.

Our daughter Eva was a very athletic type girl. She played jumping rope with other girls her age at school during recess and lunch. When it came Eva's turn, she would jump without missing for a very long time. This upset the other girls and although they tried to do things that would make her miss, she did not. The climax came when Eva jumped rope through both recesses and the noon hour and then again the next day at recess. The other girls went to the teacher because they thought this was unfair and maybe it was. In any event, the school administration asked Nobi to come to the school to discuss limiting the number jumps that Eva could take before giving the turn to other girls. This worked well during our stay at Fort Ord.

My honey decided that she was going to learn to drive and get her driving license. She was much easier to teach her to drive than it was for me to learn.

She studied the driving manuals very hard and learned quickly and soon had her learners permit. Now she could drive as long as I was in the car. I let her drive on the post and in town and she was soon ready for the Department of Motor Vehicles inspector. She knew that her first task was parallel parking, which she was not too good at, so I lined up the car so that she could easily do the parking. She did not miss many other tasks and was given her driver's license. Upon leaving the testing area after receiving her license, she took off too fast and barely missed another car. I said to her, "You missed that car by the thickness of a coat of paint, be careful sweetheart"; and she was careful always after that.

Nobi was pregnant with our fourth child but the hospital did not have an OB/GYN doctor so we had to use civilian doctors. We chose a doctor from Seaside on recommendations from friends. She went to him for regular checkups but it wasn't until much later in her pregnancy that we learned that he worked from a hospital in Salinas, CA. This was about seventeen miles away from Fort Ord and the only route to take was driving along State Highway 68 which we now know is the long way around. When I was informed that she was ready to deliver, of course it would be late at night. I helped her into our 1956 Plymouth that we had since coming from Germany and drove the seventeen miles very fast because I was afraid that the distance between the hospital and our house would take too much time. I made it with little time to spare because when I got there she was taken directly away into the delivery room (where I could not go) and prepared her for delivery. By the next morning, on November 7, 1958 we had a baby girl that we named Judy Kay. When we brought the baby home, Robert told his mother, "Mom! Take that baby back to the hospital". We had to watch him because sometimes he tried to hit the baby; however he soon got over "not being the baby".

Soon afterwards, the army engineers decided to make major renovations to the quarters at Bay View Park. We were required to move from our quarters at 388 Leinbach Ave to 398 Leinbach, about five or so houses down. After this move, we began thinking about buying our own home. We saved our money and together with another reenlistment bonus, we began looking for a house we could afford, in the location acceptable to us. We had already rejected living in Seaside where most black people were herded. We looked at several houses in the Salinas area. When we found an affordable house acceptable to us, either the banks or lending institution rejected our offer on grounds that we did not financially qualify for the loan; although white people making less money were given comparable loans. We were not discouraged though and kept looking. Then one day while I was in the bank with another soldier that worked in my office, I luckily heard the news that a man named Jones wanted to sell his house and that he lived on the side of Salinas. Without going back to the office, I went directly to Salinas to inquire about the house. When Mrs. Jones answered the door, she confirmed that they did indeed want to sell the house, but I would have to wait until her husband came home from work about five o'clock in the evening. At the appointed time, Nobi and I, hand in hand, knocked on their door. We made a deal that night to assume his loan by buying him out.

On Thanksgiving Day we moved into our new home. We were greeted with open arms by the neighbors on both sides of us as they were military people. Our neighbor on the left, Sylvan DeLost was on his roof removing leaves when he saw us. He came down immediately and we met Sylvan and Lorraine DeLost and their three children. They asked us if we needed anything or help. We declined stating we were just moving from Fort Ord. We became friends almost immediately; however I cannot say that we were too welcomed by some of the other neighbors. One woman became so upset that she moved somewhere in North Salinas. Syl and Lorraine said that they would not miss her much because this woman liked to carry gossip from house to house. We did not ever know this woman but from what Lorraine had to say about her, we did not want to know her. Syl was very good at woodworking and I learned a lot from him over the years. On the other side of our house lived a Naval Officer who was attending the Naval Postgraduate School at Monterey. He and his wife had two children who were always in our yard playing with our children. We had found a home at last, where we could raise our children. There were good schools in our area, we had ample yard our kids to play, good stores in the neighborhood and downtown was not too far away. We were central to almost everything. We could enter the freeway going north in just two blocks away. If there was a drawback to our new home, it was that I had to drive fifteen miles to work each day. We were as happy as one could be, even financially as my quarters allowance covered the house payment and some of the utilities.

At work things were going very well. The post administrators decided to consolidate all officers into one place. We were given a bigger building and I had a section of five soldiers. My immediate supervisor and I ate our lunch together and talked about any and all things. This was well and good until the Department of the Army decided to give us all proficiency test. Those in the top four percent would receive an additional allowance, amount depending upon the military occupation involved. For my job level this would be an additional thirty dollars, which I could always use raising four children. When the test was given I was in the top four percent however my immediate supervisor was not. This caused a lot of friction and lot of misinformation was tossed about. While the misinformation was soon cleared, the friction between us remained. We had strained relationship until he received orders to go overseas.

My parents decided to visit us this summer, travelling from Little Rock by plane. Nobi and I drove to San Francisco to pick them up and drive them to Salinas. When we arrived home and told Judy that these were her grandparents, she ran to my father and said, "I have a grandpa and grandma, I did not know that I had a grandpa and grandma". She kept close to her grandparents during their entire visit. It was no secret that she had grandparents; it's just that we did not discuss it much. The other children had at one time or another gone to Little Rock and knew of them. Seems as though that while at school other children talked about their grandpa or grandma and she did not know hers, so she could not say anything about them. It was such a surprise to her that she did have grandparents.

Inflation began to grip the nation, prices were rising and no promotions were forthcoming for anyone no matter how good a job one was doing. My children were growing up and needed many more things, and wanted even more things. I needed to earn more money. One of my jobs was to select officers to serve on the General Court as our court jurisdiction had increased and trials were held at least weekly. General Court Martial is trials for serious offenses i.e. murder, rape, extortion and other major crimes. I noticed that the Post Exchange officer always claimed he was too busy to serve and most of the times I skipped him on the roster. As my needs for money grew, my boldness grew in asking him for a job. Finally one day when he as asking to be excused again, I told him I needed a job and that from time to time I remade the roster and I might just inadvertently leave his name from the roster. He said he would call me back. I was apprehensive until he called me back as he could have been reporting me and I would be in trouble. When he did call me, he told me to report to a branch in the troop area to a man named Pumphrey. All he told Mr. Pumphrey was he was sending a man there and for him to hire him. What I did not know then was that Mr. Pumphrey and the exchange officer were having slight strained relationship. At first I was just getting the bare minimum of four hours per week even when there was work to be done. I sensed that he did not want me around, but had to keep me. I had been working for about two months when one night we were putting away a quite large order of merchandise. As we were working, as he opened a case of cigarettes, he forgot to adjust the blade on the box cutter and cut through four cartons of cigarettes. While he was looking dejected, I laughed. When we were alone putting the empty boxes into the dumpster, he turned to me and said, "I guess I am now in trouble with the Post Exchange Officer. He will know about the cigarettes before morning". Again I laughed and said, "I don't think so, are you planning on telling him yourself. I work for you, am loyal to you". He thought that I was put there to spy on him and reports everything that went wrong. After we had this conversation, my hours increased until I was working as many hours as I could.

One of my jobs was to process officer actions. This meant that any application submitted by any officer on the post was processed by me. One day we received in the office a copy of an Inspector General's report that was not good. This report had been reviewed by the Commanding General who had written in the margin a note directing us to start elimination proceedings. This would cause the officer concerned to be immediately separated from the service. This came to me for action. My first act was to interview the Brigade Commander to determine if there were other deeds that had been committed by the officer that should also be reported. The Brigade Commander told me that the officer was in good standing and that he thought that the officer's non-commissioned officers had let him down and that he was looking into whether or not they let him down on purpose. If he found this to be true, appropriate action would be taken on them. The only other lead I could glean from the Brigade Commander was that the officer had diabetes and was too fat. I returned to my own office with little to use to comply with the Commanding General's wishes. I next sought an audience with the Hospital Commander who also acts as the Commanders Medical Staff Officer. I asked him if I could use the fact that the officer concerned had diabetes and was too fat in an elimination proceeding application. I was told that I could not because only administrative personnel would view this application and not doctors.

I returned to my office and wrote the application with what little I had, and then went to the Inspector General's office, gave them the original copy with the Commanding General comments in the margin and received two copies to accompany the application. I made it perfectly clear what would happen with the copies I received. After the application was completed and typed in its final form by the secretary, I went to my Officer-in-Charge and told him that this was an awful weak case and that I thought that our boss, the Post Adjutant General should write a memo to the Commanding General stating that the case was too weak and should not be submitted. This request was denied and I was told to let Sixth Army return it and we would all be in the clear. I have to admit that I was not satisfied with this but could do nothing. I did however send the application with a memorandum asking that each staff officer review the application to determine if there is anything to preclude this application from being forwarded. No staff officer made any comments so the application was sent to the Commanding General for signature, then forwarded to Sixth Army. I want to say here that I did everything I could to keep this very weak application from being processed further and felt that somehow it would be trouble. I just did not know that it would be me that would get the brunt of the trouble. While we were banking on Sixth Army Headquarters to return the application, they did not and sent it on to the Department of the Army. At Officer Personnel

Actions Division, Department of the Army in Washington DC an acquaintance of our Commanding General sent everything back to him with a note saying "Bob you can't do this and sent a copy of the regulation prohibiting such action as only the Inspector General's report was the only thing committed by the officer. This regulation was not a personnel regulation of which I was familiar but one from the Inspector General's set.

Everybody who had anything to do with this action was summoned to the Commanding General's office. There was one Colonel, two Lieutenant Colonels, one Major, one Captain, one warrant Officer and me. He started with me as I had done most of the work in compiling the application. I told him all I had done and who I had talked to and what they had told me. Because I am loyal to those with whom I work, I did say that I had told my officers that the case was weak and should not have gone forward. When I got to the part where I visited the Inspector General's office and swapped copies with them, the Colonel verified my action and I was dismissed so I left. The other officers remained in his office discussing who was to blame until the finger pointing came back around to me. Now I am not there to defend myself. The commanding General wanted to reduce my rank, but the Adjutant General talked him out of it. I could not see how I was to blame but being the lowest in rank there I was the scapegoat. When the other officers got back to the office, I was called outside the building and told what the Commanding General had given me for punishment. I want everyone to read the next paragraph very carefully because no one should have to undergo such a strain.

The Warrant Officer, being the next in line from the bottom was elected to tell me my punishment, which was as follows: First my job would be taken from me and I would be reassigned to a place where I would be forced to work under someone junior to me so that I would be humiliated. Next if any two of the people who were summoned there were caught talking or any was discussing what went on in that office that day, I would be subject to court martial. I asked the warrant officer if he was sure of what the Commanding General said because I had no control over any of the others since they were very senior to me. He stated that the Adjutant General had asked him again if that was what he meant and he answered yes. This all happened on a Friday afternoon, so I was told to came back early Monday morning and receive my written orders. I went right home and told Nobi about this as I was sure that I was going to have to take punishment for all of us that were concerned. I knew that my darling wife would stand by me no matter what came.

I went to my new place of work at the Reception Station and sure enough I was assigned to work where two sergeants that were junior to me were my supervisors. I was very angry and scared. When the telephone would ring I just knew that someone had been caught talking about what had happened. I have to also point out that I was so grouchy that everyone would not get too close and rumors had it that I had struck an officer and was being hidden at the Reception Station. Of course that was not true and no one could know the truth because of the gag order. Things went on like this for over a year. My dear wife who had all her teeth removed in order to get dentures had to remain in our car for over an hour because I was too scared to ask to leave early. Then the sergeant in charge of my section received his orders to go overseas. This time the phone rang, it was someone telling me that the Station Commander wanted to see me. I knew that I was looking at a court martial with the Commanding General as my accuser. I pulled myself together and went to see what he wanted. The first thing he asked me was what went on that frightful day in the Commanding General's office. I told him I was under strict orders not to talk about it as long as General Petry commanded this post. I was then informed that General Petry had gone to Washington, DC after receiving his third star. I was so relieved that I broke down and cried like a baby. The Station Commander gave me a few moments to collect myself and we talked. When I told him exactly what had happened, he stated "That's all, you were punished so severely for making an error which was doubtful as being your error. Then he told me that he wanted me to take over the section I was working.

All during this ordeal my honey of a wife was both loving and supportive. I do not believe that I would have survived if it was not for her. My health was beginning to wane. It was during this period that I suffered the first Transient Ischemic Attack (TIA). A TIA is caused by the nerves surrounding the blood vessels to the brain are wound so tight that the circulation is temporarily cut off. I was also still working part time, after work, at the Post Exchange because our family needed the additional money I made there. In a sense this helped me because I had time to unwind before going home thereby letting me leave my troubles at work.

Prior to taking over this section initiating records of inductees into the military service, I had been so wrapped up in my own troubles that I hardly knew who did what; even though I had been there over a year. One civilian woman named Georgia Benson was supposed to be my second in command. Upon learning that I would now head this section, she had gone to the Sergeant Major and refused to work with me because of how I had been during my strained period. The Sergeant Major, who knew of me during my better days, convinced her to try to work with me for at least thirty days before quitting her job. After about a week of observing how things were going in my new section, I decided that I had to first have a long talk with Georgia. Since there was not too much space between the desks in our building, I asked her to take a walk with me as I had things I wanted to discuss with her. She told me much later that she was sure she was going to quit her job this day, but she got the surprise of her life. I told her as my assistant, starting now I wanted her to do just that. I wanted her to take charge during any of my temporary absences. As we talked I learned that my predecessor would not let her make any decisions and that he stole any idea that she had and made them his own. I told her that I did not need to do this because I believed that the better my people looked, the better I looked. I also told her that I often sought the advice of my key people before making important decisions. After our talk ended, she realized that I was a much different leader than she was used to. There was no more talk of her quitting her job and before I left there, we were very good friends.

It was now decided by the high command that the army was no longer top heavy and some promotions allocations were forthcoming. At first there were very few to the grade of Staff Sergeant E6 and above and many eligible personnel. I went before the promotion board the first month and answered army type questions for over an hour before being dismissed. I was told that only three would be promoted and I was number four on the list. The next month when I went before the board, my Colonel was a member. I was not questioned about army things, but about flying airplanes (my Colonel knew I had been flying when I was young). After about twenty minutes I was dismissed and I also was promoted.

Things went along well for a while and then we were notified that all of our military interviewers would be changed to civilian personnel. This would be alright on the surface, but this meant selecting and hiring applicants, and there was a deadline to accomplish this. This task fell mostly to Georgia Benson and me. One day I was out of the office attending to military duties when a very young applicant came for interview. Georgia interviewed her alone and was so impressed with this young woman that she hired her. When I returned to the office, she was apprehensive about telling me that she had hired this young woman. When she finally told me, I told her she was doing her job and that if she likes her, I am sure the woman would work out. This young woman turned out to be one of our best interviewers.

Things changed at the Post Exchange. First Pumphrey left on his own accord and was not fired. Mrs. Bell took over his exchange in addition to the one she already managed. She was also given the Beer Garden to manage therefore she needed experienced people to help her manage the three exchanges. I was sent to assist her in managing the Beer Garden. This was a little different in that I had to purchase some of the merchandise from local venders. When the potato chip vender came, he never had enough of the things that I sold. I would go onto the truck and try to get as many boxes of chips and pretzels as he would allow, stating always that he had to save some for the other exchanges. One day he gave me a very large jar of peanut butter. I thought nothing secretive about this gift and left it on the counter. Of course a senior executive of the Post Exchange administration paid me a visit. When he asked me about the peanut butter, I told him it was a gift from the chip vender. He became angry and told me that the vender was trying to bribe me into buying more merchandise. He also would not listen that I always wanted more of everything than he was willing to give me although I could sell more. He went back to his office and put this incident on my record.

Sometimes later we were subject to an Inspector General inspection. The three of us who were employed there worked all night making the building ready for inspection. Mrs. Bell had instructed me to have the correct monies in my safe. It was the policy of the Post Exchange to charge the patrons twenty-five cents deposit on the pitchers which was returned when they returned the pitchers. Some patrons left the pitchers outside, others left them on the tables. I had also been instructed not to ring up the money left by the pitchers not being returned. On the day of the inspection, we passed with flying colors with the exception of the money left from the pitchers not returned, as I had just left the money in a cigar box in the stock room, which was kept locked. Because of this, together with the peanut butter, this same executive instructed Mrs. Bell to fire me. I went home for a day or so and thought about it and decided that I would not take this as I could not see that I had done anything wrong. I went back and told Mrs. Bell to go down to the main office and tell them that if I did not get my job back, I would report all these little crooked things that I had ever seen done in my years of working with the Post Exchange. I am sure that this would cause an investigation of all the branches. I was hired back, but was not allowed to return to the Beer Garden, but I could keep my same pay. I did not care, since the work there was very hard and the young soldiers always played their music too loud.

Nobi had been in the country almost long enough to apply for citizenship. She enrolled in the citizenship classes at the Salinas Adult School which was held in the evenings. She studied very hard and I helped her as much as I could. As the time for testing approached, as we lay in bed, we took the study material and I drilled her with as many questions as she could handle. Soon my babe knew more about the history of America and its laws than I did. When it was time to be tested by Immigration personnel, she was ready and she passed with a high score. One would think she would get her citizenship then, but not through the courts here in Salinas because the Judge tested everyone all over again. All of the applicants who were tested before her, failed to pass. When her time came, she answered correctly every question the judge put before her. I was so proud of her. When we left the courtroom, the newspaper reporters were waiting to take pictures of the first to get their citizenship that day. Her picture appeared the next morning in the paper.

By working at the Post Exchange and my army job, we were not so tight with our finances. My sweetheart never complained when times were tough, so when Christmas came I wanted to get something really nice for her. I decided that I would get for her, her own car. I went to the Ford dealer and ordered the one I thought she would like. I had them deliver it late Christmas Eve. Almost every Christmas Eve there was some toy or another that required assembly so it was easy to tell her I had to get a tool for my assembly project. Instead, I accepted the car from the dealer and we both pushed it into the garage and place a big red bow on the hood. Christmas morning when the children were opening their gifts and she gave me my gift from her, she had a very odd look on her face when I had no gift for her. Later I told her that her gift was in the garage. When she saw the car with the big red bow on the hood, her face lit up so bright. It made me happy just to see her so happy.

John Street appears to be as straight as an arrow, but it isn't. When her car was about four months old, she was backing out of our driveway onto the street. From our driveway one cannot see very well what is coming along the street. One of our young neighbor girls was driving rather fast at the same time Nobi was backing out of our driveway. Nobi did stop in time however the girl's car barely touched our car causing the girls car to flip over two times before coming to rest fifty three yards from the impact. I was notified of the accident while at work and came immediately home, the wheels of my car barely touching the ground. When I arrived, our car was in the driveway. I examined it and could find no damage at first, but on closer look, just a smear of red paint was on the back bumper. I was then told by our neighbors that both my wife and the girl had been taken to the hospital. Upon arriving at the hospital, I first saw the girl, who was laying on a gurney using very bad language so I knew she was alright. When I found my wife, she too was laying on a gurney but looked sick. She had just fainted after seeing the girl's car turning over and coming to rest at the curb in front of the house next door. I was able to take Nobi home and after assuring her that the other girl was alright without any broken bones or anything, her face began to get its normal pleasant shape.

I worked at my Army job and for the Post Exchange for about a year more, without incident until I received orders to go to France where my next adventure would take place. When I received this news, Nobi and I had a decision to make since all of our children were in school and we did not want them disturbed. We decided that I would go alone for the full two year tour.

Chapter 8

TOUR IN FRANCE

I took a short leave at home and started for the debarkation center for my boat ride to Bremerhaven, Germany. Being of sufficient grade that I did not have to worry about pulling make work duties aboard ship, my trip was without incident. We took an overnight train to Paris where we were met by replacement stream personnel who put us on another train to Orleans. I was assigned to the Office of the Deputy for Personnel, United States Army Communication Zone Europe. This can be cut short by saying G1 Division, COMZEUR. When I arrived at my duty station, I was met by a Master Sergeant Everett Johnson who was from Little Rock and I had known his younger brothers when I was growing up. Everett was older than I so I did not know him as well as his family and younger brothers. He was the Chief Clerk of our office, an office I would later hold. I had had plenty of personnel experience, but had very little in the formation of army organizations. I had used Tables of Organizations and Equipment (TO&E) and Tables of Distribution (TD) all of my army life, however I had no experience forming such a document. I had to learn my job as well and as fast as I could.

I do not know how this happened; I guess the senior officers of our department saw something that they liked. One day I was called into the Colonel's office and was told that I was being made an action officer, which meant that I could be assigned projects. Later it meant that I would lead a team to take the troop basis submission to our next higher headquarters, which is the highest army headquarters in Europe. I was then given my first project. The army was to undergo a major reorganization in the year 1970. A field manual was being compiled outlining these changes. Everything pertaining to Installation and Supply was given to us in that that was our business. Our command was in charge of feeding, clothing and supplying all military personnel in Europe. This project entailed plans to support at least two combat American armies plus at least one allied army that would defend Western Europe in the event of war. The time was at the height of the cold war. Although I was given the project, I could call upon any staff section of the headquarters and/or discuss any thought or idea with any of the senior staff. This project was named TASTA-70 (The Administrative Support, Theater Army and was to be completed by the year 1970. I worked hard on this project and submitted some good ideas, though not all mine. By the end of the project, I had been away from my bride and family a long time and I really needed to see them. My enlistment was up after being away for about eight months so I reenlisted and took a 30 day leave and came home to see them. The bad thing about this was that I had to go back.

When I returned to France and to duty, I spent a lot of time around the crafts shop, mainly after duty hours. There was a French man that was in charge of the crafts shop and we got to know each other quite well. Most of the other soldiers, who did not bring their families or were single, spent off duty time out on the town. I did not want to do that nor did I have the money since I sent every penny the law allowed home to Nobi as I knew she needed it all to raise our children. The man in charge of the crafts shop began to complain that he could not get a day off. I guess he complained to me since I was about the only one who would listen. One day I told him that I could stay for him as I knew how to operate all the power tools. I went to Special Services and made an application to work after duty hours and was hired. After replacing the crafts supervisor for two days per week, the Photo lab supervisor wanted me to replace him for two days per week. The photo lab operator had to be able to mix the chemicals to develop film, instruct on how to safely remove film from the camera and to instruct and aid in developing film. I did not know how to do any of this but he took the time to teach me. Now I was replacing these men four days per week which gave me additional monies to send to my Honey. I had settled in pretty good in that I was always busy, except weekends and holidays. These times were still very hard on me as I wanted to be with my family, especially during the major holidays. On my way from my barracks to the crafts shop, I had to pass the club. Outside the club was a bank of slot machines. As I passed, I would select one and put in a coin, pull the handle and if I won I took my winnings and left and if I lost, which was most of the time, I continued walking to the shops. I never played these slot machines but once when I passed.

Several nights per week we would be called back to work at night because the senior officers did not have anything else to do but sit around the club at night and argue about the troop strength in various locations. In order to settle things, the Chief of Staff would always say, "find out which is right" which meant that we would have to come and research it. One of the reasons that these arguments took place was that several levels of command published the troop strength which might have been right at the time of publication. We learned that IBM was running a school in the area for computer instruction. I was fortunate to be able to go and after I completed the basic course, I asked if I could stay and complete the advanced course. After completing the advanced course, I returned to the office and over time compiled the troop strength of the entire command and put them on the computer. I made enough copies for every staff section and the command group. Each month when I made new runs, I took the old copies and burned them, thus no more night work for us.

When I am away from home, away from Nobi and the kids, I always write a letter to her, even if I have time only to write "I love you" on a sheet of paper. Weekends and holidays are extremely tough on me because I do not have my work to keep me busy. Of all the letters and things I sent to Nobi while in France, she only kept three of my letters. Because these letters survived for more than forty years since they were written, I am including them here.

VALENTIME'S DAY
14 FEBRUARY 1965

TO MY DARLING ANGEL;

BECAUSE YOU HAVE BROUGHT SO MUCH INTO MY LIFE, DARLING I SEND THIS SMALL GIFT WITH HOPES IN SOME SMALL WAY IT WILL ADD ANOTHER BRIGHT SPOT INTO YOUR LIFE. THOUGH WE HAVE BEEN ONE FOR A LONG TIME I LOVE YOU MORE THAN WHEN WE FIRST MARRIED. I HAVE ALWAYS FELT GREAT LOVE IN MY HEART FOR YOU

DEAR EVEN NOW WHEN WE ARE MILES APART. THE FACT THAT WE ARE MILES APART MEANS NOTHING BECAUSE I FEEL VERY CLOSE TO YOU. YOU HAVE ALWAYS MEANT MANY WONDERFUL AND SPECIAL THINGS TO ME.

LIKE THE DAWN THAT BREAKS INTO A NEW DAY, SO YOU CAME INTO MY LIFE. SINCE THAT TIME EACH DAY OF LIVING WITH YOU DARLING HAS MADE THAT PROMISE INTO REALITY.

IT HAS ADDED LOVE AND HAPPINESS TO THE EXTENT THAT UNDERSTANDING HAS BECOME THE BASE OF OUR MARRIAGE. YOU ALSO MEAN TO ME THE ULTIMATE IN BEAUTY LIKE THAT OF AN ANGEL. ALTHOUGH YOU ARE A LOVELY AND ATTRACTIVE GIRL, YOU ALSO ADD BEAUTY IN YOUR DISPOSITION. BEING SWEET IS A WAY OF LIFE TO YOU. YOU ARE THE MOST WONDERFUL AND SWEETEST PERSON I KNOW IN THIS WORLD. I AM SURE YOU WERE MADE IN HEAVEN AS NO ORDINARY PERSON COULD POSSESS ALL YOUR QUALITIES AND BE BEAUTIFUL AT THE SAME TIME.

BECAUSE YOU HAVE GIVEN ME YOUR LOVE MY DARLING, I AM MERRY AND VERY, VERY HAPPY. MATERIAL THINGS IS OF LITTLE VALUE WHEN COMPARED TO THE HAPPINESS I FEEL AS A RESULT OF RECEIVING YOUR LOVE. MY LOVE FOR YOU HAS GROWN FROM ONE TINY SPARK TO A FIRE THAT WILL EQUAL THE SUN. THE DEEP WONDERFUL FEELING I HAVE IN MY HERT WILL LAST AN ETERNITY. AS A RESULT I HAVE GIVEN YOU MY HEART WITH ALL THE LOVE I WILL EVER HAVE, TO KEEP AND CHERISH FOREVER. EACH BREATH OF MY LIFE, EACH PASSING THOUGHT AND EACH BEAT OF MY HEART IS FOR YOU, SWEETHEART, AS I LIVE TO LOVE YOU AND MAKE YOU HAPPY. NO TASK WILL EVER BE TOO GREAT IF IN THE END YOUR HAPPINESS PREVAILS.

ALL MY LOVE

Everett Johnson's overseas tour was up and he returned to the states. I then became Chief Clerk. It was now time to take the changes in troop strength to the next higher headquarters. Since I had not gone on this mission before, an officer with the grade of Major was the team leader. I was going along only to observe. I did attend the meetings; however I was not allowed to make any decisions this time around. Three months later, I was in charge and assembled my own team. I could ask for and receive any personnel throughout the headquarters as this was one of the most important tasks. One of the men who worked in our office was named Calvin Pierce. I was kind of friendly with Calvin not only as a coworker, but as one who I had visited in his home. Calvin asked me to select a certain female clerk typist in another division, so I did, without thinking too much about it. I was then briefed by all senior officers who had information that I should know, that would help me if I was required to make a decision upon which the information would be based. I also had a civilian, grade GS 13, who knew everything there is to know about supplies and equipment as a member of my team. I was last briefed by our Chief of Staff, General Young. Off we went to Heidelberg for one month. My travel orders were of the highest priority which would give my request for transportation immediate action. Things went well for about the first two weeks. During my meetings, nothing came up that I did not know about and our documents were being processed smoothly. Then I found out, accidently, that Calvin was having relations with the female clerk typist he asked me to request. Calvin is married to a very nice woman whom I liked and did not think he should be cheating on his wife. We all had separate rooms in the hotel. I warned him to stop or I would have to send her home (I could not send Calvin home as he was an integral part of the team and I could get anyone to do the typing). Sure enough about two or three days later I caught them again. I called home and asked for another typist and sent her home. Calvin was angry with me for a little while, but it did not affect his performance of duty. I told him he was lucky that I did not tell his wife. The session was soon over and the entire team returned to France.

 Upon returning to our home base, I went back to work and back to work at the crafts shop. One day there appeared something that had been a reviewing stand used in parades. When I asked about it, no one knew anything about it. I went out and examined it and there were several sheets of good plywood and some good pieces of lumbar. Nobody seemed to care about this thing so one evening I took a hammer and crow bar and disassembled it taking care not to damage the plywood. I put the plywood in the stock bin and labeled it with my name. One day Calvin came into the crafts shop when I was working and wanted to make a bar. From what he had as material, he could not make anything worthy of being in someone's home. I gave him enough wood and helped him make a very nice bar. We wanted to put a light inside, but was not familiar with a French switch so he blew the circuit breaker in his apartment three times before we figured it out.

One evening while at the crafts shop puttering around there was a commotion out in front of the movie theater. Seems as if the movie goers wanted to get inside but the manager would not open the theater because the projectionist was ill and did not come to work. I went outside and after asking around, told the manager that I could run the picture for him. This he doubted very much as he thought I was speaking of 16mm film. I told him that when I was a very young man, I worked at the movie theater in my home town of Little Rock and was taught to operate the projectors, As long as the booth was equipped with Peerless lamps and Simplex machines, I could run it. Knowing that his equipment was as I had stated, he decided to give me a try, but before selling any tickets, he would take me into the booth and see if I really could operate the pictures. Any projectionist knows that when you receive film from another theater, the film has not been re-wound. This is standard procedure because the new projectionist must check the film for loose splices or breaks. This is exactly what I did first, and then checked both lamps for sufficient arcs length for a complete reel; all before threading the film into the machine part. Now I was ready for him to sell tickets and he had confidence that I could handle the job. Everything went well, except for one tiny flaw. I would not wear my eyeglasses because I was vain and the distance from the booth to the screen was such that when the picture was in focus to me, it was out of focus to the audience. I had the manager stay in the booth until I had both machines adjusted into the right focus. Then everything went well and I had yet another relief job.

On my next submission to Heidelberg, Department of the Army had decreed that all like units must be structured alike. All of our depots, posts were exempt from this requirements. The only problem we were going to have was with the trucking companies. Seventh Army was given the job of structuring these because they had twenty one such companies while we only had nineteen. The problem came when they would not put a warrant officer as maintenance officer because they said they could not afford the warrants. Before I left my home base in France, I was instructed that we could not live with this problem because all of our nineteen trucking companies were always on the road hauling food, clothing, ammunition, even light aircraft, etc. between ships at both harbors and the General Depots. Failure to accomplish would severely compromise our mission. I assembled my team as usual, received my briefings and left for Heidelberg. I first tried talking to officials at Seventh Army but they would not budge from their position. After making sure my other work was processing smoothing, I thought it best to make a trip to Stuttgart to again try to change their minds. I even let them know that with so many miles per day securing the things they needed for their operations would be in jeopardy. Still no luck, but I did learn that even though some of their companies should have been equipped with tractor and trailers, many were equipped with 2 ½ ton trucks. This gave me a plan which I executed when I returned to Heidelberg. I wrote a request for exemption stating that all nineteen of our truck companies were equipped with tractor and trailers and that most of the ones assigned to Seventh Army Support Command, who had been given the job of structuring these companies were equipped with 2 ½ ton trucks and that to accomplish our primary mission of providing logistics to all troops in Europe, the maintenance warrant was germane to our operation. Department of the Army bought our request and we were able to keep our trucks running. When I returned home with this victory, I received high praise.

No one had been promoted for quite some times, so now finally a rather large promotion allocation was distributed to every command of the army. At this time I happen to be leading a team at Heidelberg. Almost every eligible personnel went before the promotion board and the allocation was used up promoting the top personnel. One thing I have learned is that when one is performing above his own level, others think of him as being at that level. In other words, before I started leading the troop basis team, an officer the grade of Major was the team leader. Because I was not physically present at the time recommendations were made for these promotions, I was never considered because they thought of me as already being above these grades. Needless to say, I was not among those promoted to the next higher grade. Again I am lucky to have a good friend by the name of Porterfield. My friend Porterfield worked for the Deputy for

Operations, Forces Structure Branch. He called me at Heidelberg and told me what had happened and told me that he was going to bring to the attention of the senior staff the mistake they had made. He told me he did the following: Because we work with so much classified material, we are not allowed to place documents in desk drawers, so Porterfield began to clear his desk in the middle of the morning and placed his classified material in the safe. He then sat at his desk, pulled out the middle drawer, and slammed it shut making a loud noise. His colonel sat opposite him turned and ask him what was wrong. He replied, "It's a crying shame, it's really a crying shame". His colonel asked him, "What is". He then said, "You know Sergeant Washington is up in Heidelberg fighting our battles, and if anyone should be promoted, it should have been him". His colonel got up from his desk and went immediately to see the Deputy for Operations, who called my boss, the Deputy for Personnel. Since all of the promotion allocations were used up, our Commanding General called the Commander in Chief in Heidelberg and somewhere dug up an allocation for me. There was a senior officer who still demanded that I appear before a promotion board, so my board was made up of the Chief of Staff, the Deputy for Personnel and the Deputy for Operations. My promotion was announced that day and made my date of rank the same as those promoted the day before. I often wonder if Porterfield had not made them aware of overlooking one of their more deserving persons, how long would I have had to wait before being promoted.

During the Christmas holidays, the children from the orphanage on the outskirts of Orleans came to sing for us. They sang beautifully and we enjoyed their concert very much. When it was over, they invited us to come and visit them. The invitation may have been a courtesy invitation however some of us decided to take them up on it and I am glad that we did. Before I continue, I want to outline the conditions surrounding our camp. We have about 400 of us who live at the base, however about 1500 work and eat there over the noon hour. In addition, there is a commissary there and rather than fruits and vegetables which go bad and have to be discarded, they are given to the troops which in most cases means the 400 of us that live there. There is so much food there that one may pass through the mess hall at any time of night and get something to eat. We made the visit to the orphanage and found conditions there deplorable according to our standards. The priest said that the French Government gave him very little money to operate the orphanage. They did not have wash basins for the children to wash but something similar to a horse trough where water ran from the high point to the lower. When we left to go back to base, we discussed their problem and decided to do something. Every Friday afternoon we noticed that the mess management sergeant had a group of soldiers loading a ¾ ton truck with milk and other perishable foods. We asked him what he was going to do with all of that food and he said it was being taken to be destroyed. The small group of us that had been to the orphanage went to the Company Commander and asked him if we could donate the food that was going to be destroyed to the orphanage. This being against army regulations, the Company Commander could not give us permission. He did tell us that he was not looking into what happened to the food being destroyed unless some soldier came to him and told him he was hungry. Knowing that these conditions were next to being impossible, each week we were given the food for delivery to the orphanage. Because there was so much of it, the priest did not have to spend much money for food, so he began to make other conditions better. We also convinced the commander of an Engineer Battalion to grade a baseball diamond there as a training exercise. This commander also made other repairs for the orphanage also as training exercises.

This Christmas I tried to find the appropriate gift to send to my honey; one that I could afford, and yet be something that I believed that she would like and cherish. I could not find such a gift though I look everywhere in and around Orleans France. Since I could not find what I wanted, I decided to write the following:

A GIFT OF MYSELF

MERRY CHRISTMAS MY DARLING—Over the years I have always had a gift for you, some being very expensive, others not so expensive. Though I paid nothing for this gift, money could never buy it nor is it only for Christmas time of the year but is meant to last forever. This gift of which I speak is—

MY GIFT OF LOVE—This is my most precious and most generous gift. I give you my heart and all the love that it contains. Love also means sharing so as I share my love and my life with you, I hope that you will share yours not only with me, but with everyone around you. On every Christmas Day we should remember that on this day CHRIST was born. He loved us all so much that on the Friday before Easter he died for all of us. No human being will ever be able to match this love however we should all try. Each day in my letters I reaffirm my love for you my darling. I hope and pray that when I come home I will continue to do this in both words and deeds.

MY GIFT OF UNDERSTANDING—This is more your gift to me than my gift to you, my darling, because without your love and understanding, our wonderful family would not be so close. This is one of the areas where I have shortcomings as it is hard for me to understand that which falls short of being perfect, especially if the thing is not as I want it to be. I know that my patience is short but as long as you are close to me, you will understand and make me do that which is right. I can only promise to try to listen to you and try to understand others and accept them as they are.

MY GIFT OF TIME—My time is yours. We always think we have lots of time for everything. I have spent many, many hours working trying to earn a decent living for all of us—so engrossed in this that I did not have time for my dear wife and children. Many a day have I wished I had spent much more time with the children? The most recent time was when I read your letter telling me that our youngest child will soon not believe in Santa Claus. I remembered seeing a picture of a little boy and girl asleep in an overstuffed chair trying to wait up for Santa. This made me realize that time is passing fast, and that these times are almost gone. The childhood days of all our children will have gone forever and I will have missed most of them. The times I did get to spend with them are impressed deeply into my mind and I will remember and will cherish these thoughts always. I began this article of my gift saying, "My time is yours". All that is left I hope to spend with you.

MY GIFT OF APPRECIATION AND REMEMBRANCE—My most cherished possession is the remembrance of the wonderful life that I have had because of you. I have tried in many ways to show my appreciation of you, but least of these ways I have tried the simple way of just telling it to you. I appreciate you being the sweetest and most wonderful wife in the world, and for a wonderful family, who I know is the real reason for our living. I remember all the sweet and wonderful things you have done for us all; of your sorrows and your joys. I must mention too that I have known of things you have wanted for yourself but would not ask or mention them when you thought we could not afford them. Maybe I have not gotten all of them for you yet, but as we could afford them it gave me great pleasure to give these things to you. Maybe I was a little selfish in keeping this joy to myself however I will not even try to defend this selfishness for I will do it over and over again. My appreciation for you is as my love for you. It cannot be fully expressed in mere words alone because with it comes a deep wonderful feeling from within my heart.

MY GIFT OF HAPPINESS—This is my last gift, my dearest, but not the least of these. It also comes wrapped in a bright package with a big bow. I like to think that this is my gift to you, but in reality again it is yours. It is through watching you and our children being happy that I get my own happiness. Because I love you so much and because I always want you to be happy, I give you your own way with most things however, I know our real happiness is obtained through our overflowing love for each other. As long as this condition exists, we will be able to meet every challenge of life.

So my precious wonderful darling on this and preceding pages is my gift to you this Christmas. As for our agreement not to buy a present for each other again this year, I did not pay one penny for it however I hope that throughout our lives together you will keep this gift of my thoughts of you. It is by loving that we are loved; understanding others that we are understood and through making others happy that we gain happiness.

ALL MY LOVE

From your Husband who thinks the
Whole world of you...

After Christmas I went back to work getting ready to take the next submission to Heidelberg and working at the crafts shop. There were some school teachers who taught the children of Americans living in the area around Orleans France. One came into the craft shop and wanted help in making a cabinet that would fit a particular area in her apartment. This meant going to her apartment and taking measurements. I agreed to go with her to her apartment and when we got there I immediately started making the necessary measurements and began to tell her how much material she would need and the cost of such material. Since she was going to paint the cabinet I told her that I could get her some slightly used plywood at a much reduced price. She looked at me and said, "You're married, aren't you?" I told her that I was, but asked how she could tell since I did not wear rings. She said, "You haven't tried to make a pass at me". Although this woman was very pretty, I told her that I had a beautiful woman at home who I loved very much, and that if she could wait for me until I came home, I could wait until I could go home. To that she said that there were not many like me.

I do not remember anything happening during the next two submissions to Heidelberg. I must have been very busy with my regular work, my work at the crafts shop and photo lab, with the movie theater as well as with the small group working with the orphanage. I knew that my time during this overseas tour would be coming to completion soon and that we wanted the orphanage to be self-sustaining when we were gone.

The next submission, which would be my last one, had a very big problem. The Department of the Army had issued some very new missiles to Seventh Army. These missiles required special personnel who would perform depot type maintenance on these missiles. The special personnel were not available and could not be added to the appropriate Tables of Organization of a unit under our command. The real reason that we could not make the additions was that the Department of the Army did not also issue the necessary resources required. Every Commander had reason to be concerned, since the Soviet Union was making lots of noise about invading Western Europe and if such an event did take place, these missiles would be needed in its defense. Unrelated to the problem, it just so happened that we were ordered to inactivate an engineer battalion, since it was no longer needed, leaving just enough resources to solve the problem with the missiles. One might think we could just solve the missile problem with the resourced left from the inactivation of the engineer battalion. Unfortunately we had been ordered to turn these resourced in. As I prepared for my last mission, every staff section I visited for instructions, including the Chief of Staff, each asked me to see if I could have the spaces from the inactivation reissued back to us in order to plow these spaces into the missile problem. I assembled my team and began my journey to Heidelberg. After making sure that my team was processing our documents smoothly, I worked on my plan to retrieve the spaces. My plan was to ask each of the staff sections here to write me a memo stating their support in issuing the spaces back to us in order to solve the problem with the missiles. I started executing my plan with first going to Munitions and Missiles, then to Deputy for Operations and then to Deputy for Personnel. Armed with these memorandums of support, I could then write a formal request for the spaces. Well so much for my plan because when I went to my first stop, a Captain came to the counter and after I told him who I was and what I wanted, he told me that they would support such a plan and to wait. I thought he was going to get the memo written and typed. I waited and I waited until I was sure something was wrong and I started to leave, but the Captain soon returned and asked me to accompany him.

We went through his office and into the office of the chief, a general officer. He asked me to tell the general what I had told him. After identifying myself to him, I told him that my command had been ordered to inactivate an engineer battalion, organize two engineer companies and to turn in the remaining resources. I also told him I had asked for a memo from him giving his support to a plan to have the spaces reissued back to us so that they could be plowed into the missile problem. The general asked me if I brought documents that contained the specialized personnel. I told him that I had not because if we could get the spaces, they would be put in documents on the next submission three months later. He then asked me if Department of the Army in Washington DC was to receive the spaces that would be turned in. I told him that as far as I knew, the spaces would remain here in Europe. I could tell that he was not happy with waiting that long, so he telephoned the Commander of US Army Advanced Weapons Support Command, our unit responsible for the support of these missiles, and told him to get the Tables of Organization and Equipment ready with all of the required specialized personnel in the proper places within the document, and that the Captain and I would be there to get them as soon as we could drive to Kaiserslautern to get them.

As we left his office, the Captain and I went outside to get the car while he went towards the command building. All the way to Kaiserslautern and back I worried about this because I could not submit these documents without the resource spaces that I did not have. I came to the conclusion that he could make me go and get the documents, but he could not make me submit them, even though

I wanted to do so, but with the resources. When the Captain and I returned to Heidelberg, it was dark. The captain went to turn in the car while I went to lock everything in the office that was provided to us. As I was unlocking the office door, I heard someone call my name but I could not see them because I was under a light over the door and whoever was calling my name was still in the dark. When this person stepped into the light I said, "Oh! Barrett", as it was Master Sergeant Barrett and another sergeant who weighed in at over 300 pounds. Barrett immediately asked me to give him the TO&E's (Tables of Organization and Equipment). I knew he could not have known that I had been sent to Kaiserslautern for them, so I asked him, "What TO&Es are you talking about". At this point the 300 pound sergeant began to inch closer to me. I could not move back because I was already against the door jam. Barrett then said, "Don't play dumb, you know very well what TO&Es". I knew something was wrong and I should not give him the documents, but still for him to be acting in such a threatening mode, someone with lots of power was guiding his actions. Still I felt that I should not give him the documents, because I had worried both going and coming from Kaiserslautern over this same action. I did not have the resources and to give these documents to him voluntarily would place my command out of balance by one hundred and fifty spaces. Barrett asked me again for the documents and I could not stall further, and it appeared that he knew about the TO&Es, so I told him that I had not checked them over. He said, "I'll do it for you". All the times I had been working with him, he had never volunteered to do my work. The 300 pound sergeant was so close to me he was touching my chest when Barrett asked again for the documents and again I stalled, "I have not run the Standard of Grades or anything" and again Barrett said that he would do it for me. In frustration, I gave him the TO&Es and as I did so, I said to him, "You know that I do not have the spaces for them". He then told me not to worry about the spaces. The 300 pound sergeant said that it was a good thing that I gave them the documents because if I didn't, they were prepared to take them away from me. When I went to my hotel, even though I was very tired, I did not sleep well worrying about what had happened and the repercussions that could come from it. At this point I was very confused as to who could have such power to make these two act with such threatening force and why.

The next morning when I went in to work, no one said a word about the TO&E's or what had happened the night before. Two more days passed and again not a word was said. I began to feel a little at ease and maybe it was going to be as Barrett had said, "not to worry about the spaces". Just as a smile was beginning to return to my face I met this two-star general by the name of Gray in the hallway. I greeted him with the customary, "Good Morning sir", and kept on walking. He called me back and asked me, "Aren't you that sergeant who is the leader of the team from COMZ", and I confirmed that I was and he asked me if I had turned the spaces in yet. I did not know what to tell him as I did not know who had ordered the business with the TO&Es, so I thought it best to tell him the truth as I knew it. I told him that I had not and that it was one of the last things done before I returned to France. I was in the process of trying to tell him why that was when he lit into me something fierce and ordered me to go and turn the spaces in immediately. He asked me if I understood and I told him, "Yes sir". He turned and went back into his office, but I just stood there as I was totally confused now and did not understand any of what was going on.

As I pulled myself together, I said to myself that I had better go and turn in the spaces. As I was walking toward Barrett's desk, I was passing the secure telephones when the sergeant there popped out and said, "Ah! Washington, I was just coming to look for you, your commander is on the phone for you". I stopped and took the call from my commander who asked me what was going on. I did not have a good answer for him and told him about being so confused about the orders and actions that had taken place in the past few days. He then told me that General Gray was threatening to have me court-martialed if I did not turn in the spaces today. He further cautioned me to stay as far away from him as possible as he was very angry with me and that he (my commander) could not protect me as he was not there in Heidelberg with me. I was not even to walk past his office, and if I had to go that way, go around the building to get to where I needed to go. He then asked me what I was going to do and I told him that I was on my way to turn in the spaces. We rang off and I went to meet with Barrett. When I arrived at Barrett's desk, the 300 pound sergeant was there also. When I asked for the TO&E's back, they both laughed a smug laugh at me and said that they knew something I did not know.

I told them that I was very serious and that if I did not get back the TO&E's and he issued a voucher taking the spaces from me, I was going to get court-martialed. The smug grin left his face and he said that we should go into Colonel Detlie's office. After bringing Colonel up to speed on the happenings, he call the Deputy for Personnel on the phone and Informed him that I, the representative from COMZ had made a formal request for the TO&E's return. The Deputy instructed us to do nothing until he got back to us as he was going to see the chief. When the Deputy called us back, this is what he told us: He said that the Commander-in-Chief had said, "Under no circumstances are you to give him back the TO&E's" and repeated these instructions. When the deputy asked him if he was going to tell General Gray that it was his instructions on how to use the spaces and he said, "No, I cannot go against my senior officers". The Deputy then said, "Then you are going to let Washington stand trial". To this he said, "You are all smart boys, solve the problem. I do not want to hear any more about this".

When I heard this I was so distraught that I found myself yelling at the top of my voice, "What does he want from me", "What does he want from me, I am only trying to serve my commander the best that I can". I pulled myself together and asked this same question and was told that General Gray was promised 19 of the spaces when I turned them in to activate a small unit on the Italian Rivera, (a general officer perk). Everything became crystal clear then, the General in charge of Munitions and Missiles had gone directly to the Commander-in-Chief, and told him that he had the ability to solve the missile problem, and that he had sent me and one of his officers to Kaiserslautern to get the TO&E's prepared. I said that I would give him the 19 spaces, so this is how we smart boys solved the problem. I had 5 spaces that had been taken out of other documents as not being necessary or the justification for such additions was not approved. Barrett said that he had 6 more of the same that he had not told me about. Colonel Detlie said that he would give me the remaining 8 spaces for the total of 19 that were needed. He then instructed Barrett to get a General Order issued activating the unit in Italy, issue a voucher taking from me the 11 spaces that I gave up and after the order was issued to take a copy to General Gray. After all of this, General Gray tried to joke with me the next morning and I had to smile and acknowledge the joke.

Sometimes, even now I have dreams of this episode (I have been retired from the army 41 years as of the time I am writing this).

The only difference in my dreams is that I am defending myself in a general courts-martial. I open my testimony by stating that sometimes we describe a situation that is not factual but easier to say. A good example is that we say, "the sun is rising or the sun is setting" when in fact a given point on the earth surface is revolving toward the sun or in case of a setting sun, the point is revolving away from the sun. In this case, a space has no substance and cannot be handled so the act of turning them in is accomplished by this headquarters issuing a voucher relieving me of the spaces. My only responsibility is to demonstrate that the spaces are clear from documentation; otherwise I have no further control. I can see that the court start talking among themselves and want verification so they call Colonel Detlie who verifies everything I have testified. Since no verdict can be reached I usually awake.

The next three weeks passed without problems and when I returned to my home base, no one said one word about the incident. I thought someone would either tell me I had done a good job; or if they thought differently, that I did not handle it right, but to say nothing left me without any guidance. Another thought being that maybe there was nothing to say in that the whole thing was under the authority of the Commander-in-Chief and there was not anything anyone could say.

My tour in France was nearing the end. I had just finished writing my daily letter to my sweetheart telling her that this will be my last letter; when I heard a knock at my door. Upon answering it, there stood an officer in the grade of major. I did not know him so I asked him, "Sir, may I help you". He asked me if I was the Sergeant Washington who was an Action Officer and I told him that I was. He then asked to see my identification card that all military personnel had been issued and required to carry. I went to my billfold and got my identification and showed it to him. He then went into his wallet and showed me his. After we each had been properly identified, he said to me, "I want you to go to your office, unlock the safe and bring back a listing of all units, their location and strength". I also want you to bring a document outlining all units' organizational structure." Without hesitation I said, "Sir, you know that both documents are classified". He acknowledged that he knew that the documents were classified so I asked him if he would mind going down to the company office and give me the order in the presence of the Duty Officer. He said, "No, the fewer people who know of this, the better".

In this large headquarters where we all worked, one of the few offenses for which one will be in serious trouble is to mishandle classified documents. The command is so strict in the handling of classified documents that we are not allowed to place classified documents into any desk drawer. We are provided with boxes for them and upon leaving our desk even for lunch and especially after duty hours, we are required to place these boxes into the safe. Also at the end of each day, two officers are detailed to visit each desk in the headquarters, including the desk of the Commanding General, to see if a classified had been inadvertently left in the desk. One can see why I was reluctant to go and take a classified document from the safe at night without knowing how it is to be used or where it will be taken. When I asked the major where we would be taking the documents, he said that he could not tell me. My mind was working overtime as to wonder if I wanted to be in trouble for disobeying a superior officer or mishandling classified documents. At this point my mind was favoring disobeying a superior officer.

I tried one more time by asking him who else would be going to the unknown place with these classified documents. I was happy that he began to name people with whom I often worked so I told him I would go and get the documents. To get to my office, I had to walk through the parade field. This long walk made me again wonder about this adventure. At night there is a guard on each of the general staff offices so I had to produce identification and sign-in on a log stating why I was entering the building. Because I was still not too sure about what we were about to do, I signed-in and the reason for entering the building, I entered, "To remove classified documents under orders". The guard looked at my entry and frowned but had no authority not to let me in. I went to my office and retrieved the documents and returned to where the major waited. He took me into the command building to a large room on the third floor. This room also had a guard on the door only this time one entering could not leave until the exercise was completed. I was then told that we were going to plan the movement of all army units from France and move them into either Belgium or Germany.

I said to myself, "Oh God, another big project and I am about to go home".

My good friend Porterfield and I were the only two enlisted men on the project. There were several large four foot by eight foot panels on the wall with each unit located in France that plans had to be made for, taking into consideration the number of dependents associated with each unit and the location and availability of schools. When we began, the officer in charge would give a general description of the new area and my job was to select the unit that would be a good fit. Others would then indicate the actual strength of the unit, the number of dependents associated. I have to admit I felt inadequate for this job since so much was at stake. I thought if I could be lucky enough to only place the easier units until morning, I was sure that Colonel Davis, our boss would send a senior officer to take over and that since I could not leave, I could be used to look up data for him and the pressure would be off of my back. I was really worried about the General Depots and the Ammunition Depots since they were such large units and I might have to break them up and I also knew that we had a General Depot in Germany, so where would I put another. Well luck was somewhat with me because when my watch indicated that it was eight o'clock, (after a while you could not tell if it was day or night because the panels were over the windows). When nine o'clock came I wondered when my replacement would come so I called over to the office and was told that when Colonel Davis asked who was on the project and was told that I was, he said, "He will do alright, no need to send anyone else". I was grateful for the confidence that they had for my abilities. It took us three whole days and nights to complete this project. I needlessly worried about the depots as they were moved intact and was the easiest to move. When the project was completed it was two days past the time for me to leave France and go home to my honey, so I packed my bags and obtained a port call by phone. The port personnel also belonged to our command so it was easy to be accommodated but they told me not to come empty handed, this meant to bring something in a bottle. I gathered up all my unused alcohol I had in my room and went and bought two more bottles because as soon as I arrived at Frankfurt I wanted to be on the first plane out. I was to be assigned to the 5th Infantry Division at Fort Carson, Colorado. When I arrived at McGuire Air force Base/Fort Dix New Jersey, I wasted little time being processed and was on my way to Salinas and my family.

    After the niceties of being home were over, Nobi and I start planning on how to move the family to Fort Carson, Colorado. We were sure that there had been many changes since being there earlier in our lives. Our children were all in school so this is one consideration that we had to iron out. James was in High School and was an integral part of the team so they wanted him to remain in Salinas until the season was over. He was to stay with one of his friends with the approval of his parents, so we allowed him to stay and provided him with transportation to join the family after the season. Friends of Syl and Lorraine next door wanted to rent our house while we were gone. We knew this would be alright since Syl and Lorraine vouched for them and knew them well. We packed our belongings to be shipped to Colorado and about a week to ten days before my leave was up, we departed by car to our new home.

Chapter 9

OUR STAY AT FORT CARSON

We arrived at Fort Carson on Halloween. Because we had been to Fort Carson and Colorado Springs before, we decided to try for post housing first. To our surprise we were lucky and were assigned housing on the post. We moved in that day with the things we brought from home in Salinas and the things furnished by the government. We spent the day putting our things away and getting our house in order so that our lives would not be disrupted by the move. James, Eva and Robert went out "trick or treating" during the evening hours. In doing so they ran around without taking too much notice of where they lived since they were new to the area. When they had finished, they were lost and had to be escorted home by the military police. They were not in any trouble and the military police were happy to bring them home. We all laughed about it.

When I reported for duty, I was assigned to the 19th Artillery Battalion as Personnel Staff NCO. I thought this was strange since there was a master sergeant already doing the same job. I soon found out that the Colonel commanding the battalion was not too stable. No one was happy there, even the officer personnel. Anytime that I told the colonel anything that he did not want to hear, I would be fired and the master sergeant would take over the job. That is until he told the colonel something he did not want to hear and he would be fired. Being fired meant that you would go over to the company headquarters and help the first sergeant. After being fired two times, I asked my friends to move me to another unit. I was assigned to the 21st Artillery Battalion. Here everyone was happy and did their jobs willingly. This battalion had Honest John Missile as the primary weapon. When I reported in for duty, I made it clear that I did not drink coffee therefore I did not make coffee. One day the troops were all out in the field training and no one was left in the headquarters but the Colonel and me. The colonel was rumbling around in his office wanting a cup of coffee, but would not come out and ask me to make some. When I got tired of him fussing to himself, I decided I would try to make him a cup. I had no idea how much fresh coffee grounds to put in the big coffee urn, so I decided that since the place where the fresh coffee went was full, I should fill it again after dumping out the used. When the coffee finished percolating, I took a cup in to him. He thanked me but I could tell something was wrong because my coffee was thicker than that left in the urn. I thought that if I was going to be in a rocket unit, I should learn something about the rocket. Some classes were being held in the building that housed the rockets so I went to try and learn something. I learned that all of the components of the rocket warhead have dark colors except one piece and if you did not want to be blown to bits, one would not fool around with this piece. So ends everything I ever learned about the rocket.

As a rule I did not have to go to training exercises out in the field. One field trip I learned that they were going to live fire one rocket. I wanted to see this, so I went for three days in the field just to see them fire the rocket. On the last night there in the field, when it was time to fire the rocket, everyone was standing around in anticipation of the firing. The troops had everything ready so when the time came and the order was given to fire, that rocket took off from the launcher and was gone out of sight in a flash. A few minutes later, a great flash could be seen far away. I have to say that I was impressed.

Just as I was settling down into a routine at my job, I received orders to go to Camp Perry, Ohio on temporary assignment for the National Rifle and Pistol matches. I was to be in charge of the Ordnance Detachment, the gun specialist that kept the rifles and pistols in tip top shape. I did not know that the people who were in charge of the commissary were trying to get the administration to place an administrator in charge of the dining hall because the job required the disbursement of funds that was not familiar to the mess personnel. Being a premier administrator, I was assigned this job. This made me angry, I do not know why, but it did, and I did not want to do this job. I think maybe my feelings were hurt because I thought that the job was beneath my talents. In any event, the commanding officer told me in no uncertain terms that I would be assigned the job. I went to the mess hall and the first thing I did was slamming the door off the hinges and made the engineers come and fix it. A few days passed with nothing to do, but on the following Monday morning, I had to have breakfast for one thousand hungry men ready and I did not know how to get anything like food. All I had was a very clean kitchen and dining hall with no personnel. My cooks were to come over the weekend and I was told that a Warrant Officer would be there to help. I received the cooks over the weekend but I was still looking for the warrant officer. I looked in the telephone book for something like a class 1 supply as I knew that these are the people who issue food. There was no class 1 supply in the telephone book; only the commissary. I decided I would go ask the people at the commissary where I could go to get food supplies for my mess hall. I was surprised to learn that these people were delighted to see me and was happier still that their suggestion had become a reality.

The civilian man in charge of the commissary took me into his office and helped me make out all the necessary forms to have funds transferred into my account so that I could buy everything that I needed; and to pay the milk and bread vendors who would deliver these goods daily. This idea was to save the government thousands of dollars over the course of the summer. Late Sunday afternoon when all of my cooks were present, I asked each of them their qualifications and was surprised to learn that these reservists were also chefs and cooks in large hotels and were used to producing very good and tasty food. I then gave them my instructions on how this kitchen was to be run. I only had three rules: (1) the food was to look good. (2) The food was to taste good and (3) there was to be plenty of it. I also told them that I did not know or care about the rules the army required and that they could do anything they thought necessary to achieve the three rules I had outlined. Needless to say we had a swell breakfast the next morning and everyday all summer.

The next day I received some Navy Stewards so I had then to serve the senior NCOs. Seems I was running a very good dining hall as the number of people I was feeding began to grow by at least fifty more than the one thousand that I was to feed. I checked with the first sergeant who told me that we had not gotten any additional troops. I had to then check everyone who entered my establishment.

I thought things were running smoothly only to be called to the commissary and be told that the milk vendor was worried that I was not rotating my milk because every day I just told him to put the milk in the walk-in cooler. He then taught me how to read the milk code and asked me to go and check my milk for any that was outdated. I learned that I had fifty cases that had to be destroyed and another thirty-five cases that had to be used almost immediately. I could not wait to report this to the commanding officer and say to him, "see I told you I did not know what I was doing". He told me that I was not the only one who had destroyed milk and that I was doing a fine job and for me to stop complaining. To use the milk that was nearing its "use by" date I kind of lied to the troops. I told them as they was in line to enter that the dietitian had said that they were not drinking enough milk and that each man would take at least two cartons and more if they wanted.

When I was first assigned this job, I was told that I did not have to touch the food. I noticed that on Fridays, every other week, I was short some cooks. Since I am one who will always help my personnel, I found myself frying chicken in a very large kettle fryer. One day while I was doing this, the commanding officer came through my kitchen and saw me. Of course I just had to say something smart to him like "Yea You will never have to touch the food". He just laughed and kept on walking. Another day I was removing steaks from their carton when I noticed that some of the cartons had a plastic bag among the steaks. Without looking, I just placed these bags into my freezer and over time I had a freezer full. While at the commissary talking about other things, I mentioned that I ought to have better steaks because there was a plastic bag with something in it that was taking the place of some of my steaks. He just laughed and told me to go and thaw one out. I was very surprised that these plastic bags held Filet Mignon and I had a freezer full. I decided to have a party for the troops after the evening meal, so I had the cooks place the filets on trays to thaw and prepare some potato salad and other condiments suitable for a party. There was a bar-be-q pit in an open space so this where we had the party. Everyone had a good time relaxing from the daily routine.

About the middle of the summer some sergeants whom I had become friendly with thought that we needed a drink. We had heard talk that there was a joint a few miles along the highway. When we found the place there were too many people there so the proprietor was screening everyone he let in. I gathered that no one was giving their true name because of the kind of joint it was but you could still get something to drink there, but not in the camp. When my time came, he asked my name and I told him, "Robert Stone". He said, "OK Stone, fifty cents, sign the book and go on in". I guess no one else had tried to use that name. I did not stay long as I soon really found out what kind of a joint it was. I am sure that my sweet wife would not approve.

We lived next door to a man who sometimes went hunting. One day he had killed a large deer and he asked me to help him dress it out. We hung it up so that the blood would drain on Saturday evening and on Sunday we worked all day stripping the fir and butchering it into manageable pieces for cooking.

After we had finished, I was permitted to take what meat I wanted and he put the balance into his freezer. I took mine into the house and put mine into our freezer. I guess about two weeks passed before I decided to cook venison steaks for us for dinner. I had no idea that my sweetheart would not eat game or let us eat it. I went to the freezer for it and could not find any of the meat that I had placed there. I asked Nobi what had happened to my meat and she said, "You mean that mess you put in the freezer two Sundays ago, I cooked it and gave it to the dog". I did not know what to say; we did not own a dog so she must have given it to the neighbors' dog. From this day on, I never brought home any type game even though I had been offered it several times while there in Colorado where our neighbors went hunting all during the season.

Fort Carson lies on the east side of the great Rocky Mountains and it get very cold in the winter. Also sometimes it gets very windy. One very windy morning Nobi was trying to take Judy to school which was not very far from our quarters. The wind was blowing so hard that morning that it moved the big dumpsters. As they were walking toward the school, for every step they took, they were blown back two steps. They were not making any headway until the military police patrol saw the predicament they were in and took them to the school. Nobi stared at the school until the wind died down a bit before going back home.

James was on the football team of the little high school that lies on the edge of Fort Carson in the small town of Fountain, Colorado. All of the Fort Carson high school aged children went to this school. The year that we were there, they seem to have a very good team.

At the beginning of the season, they played one of the big schools in Colorado Springs to a 7 all tie. They went unbeaten the rest of the season and then it was time to play their longtime rival. This team had beaten them the year before to spoil their unbeaten record for the year. The game went well for our side and by the third quarter the game was out of reach so the coach pulled the first team and began playing reserves. Our reserves played well and did not let the other team score until the last few minutes of the game. Our boys began thinking of the year before and did not want their rivals to get the score so the first team pestered the coach to send them back in to prevent the score. The very next play a freak accident occurred that no one could understand how it happened. The play was nothing more than a dive play over tackle but when it was over one of our players was laying on the ground with a big hole in his helmet. I was the first one to the scene because I hopped over the short fence and ran out on the field. A knee could not have made the hole in this boy's helmet or the damage it did to the boy. When we left Colorado, this child was still in the hospital so we do not know the final outcome of his injury.

As I said before, the high school was very small. They could never get 300 students there at one time. The same boys, who played football, also ran track or field any team that the school participated. It was during track season that James, who was their long jumper, would take a good jump on his first try and would not take any more unless he was beaten. This did not sit well with the coach because it showed James was not trying to do his best. One time as James was making his first jump; he jumped over the confines of the pit and skinned his knee very badly. He had to be taken to the hospital at Fort Carson. It was not long after this that James and some of the other boys were in trouble with the school. It was during the time where the peace symbol was displayed and the school administration thought that displaying this symbol meant participating in the use of dope. Of course this was not true to these boys as they were the cream of the crop, all athletes. The trouble began when one of the boys purchased with his own money a suit that contained a necklace with the peace symbol as the centerpiece. When he wore this outfit to school, the administration suspended him so each of the other members of the team also made makeshift outfits with the peace symbol and wore them to school hoping for the same punishment or just to show solidarity. To make peace with the school, all of the fathers got together and went to the school to talk with the principal because we thought that to brand a kid with using dope just because of his clothing was ridiculous. All of the boys returned to school. The Christmas season came and we all piled into the car to go look for a nice Christmas tree. We visited several tree farms as we wanted a freshly cut tree that we cut ourselves. All of the trees were either too large; or too small; or too skimpy; or too expensive. Even the children who really wanted to have a tree did not find one that they liked. On the way back home, we stopped in a Walgreen drug store in Colorado Springs looking for other sundries. There on a stand stood an artificial tree just the right size. Even the children thought it was just right so we purchased it for $7.95 which was much cheaper than any we saw at the tree farms. We used this tree while at Fort Carson; brought it home to Salinas and to this day we are still using it, though it is getting a little worn. I would guess that we got our money's worth out of this little tree. After I returned to Fort Carson following the summer tour at Camp Perry, I had been awarded the Army Commendation Medal for my work in France and was to be given at a parade. I did not tell Nobi that I was going to get a medal at a parade that day and was surprised and proud that my commander had sent someone to my house and brought her to the reviewing stand to see the parade. I was so proud when the Executive Officer read the citation along with the letters that had been sent from Camp Perry attesting to the good job that I had done there. I was equally proud when the troops passed in review and saluted my medal. Summer turned to fall and the start of the high school football season began. The boys that had fielded the team last year were for the most part the same. The team got off to a good start beating their much lesser opponents. It was near the end of the season when they had to play their rivals and of course the teams that were harder to beat.

 I would like to say that all was well, especially for James as I received orders to go to Vietnam. The team wanted James to remain there under supervision of some of the parents of the team. Nobi and I had been asked by these moms several times. While we were making up our minds whether to allow him to stay, James told us that he wanted to go with the family back to Salinas so the decision was then easy for us.

 I knew that I would be going into a combat zone and that I might be seriously wounded or killed. Although we were doing well financially now, we had to assure that the family would have enough money to at least see the children through high school and for Nobi for the rest of her life. I knew that the military insurance would only provide fifteen thousand dollars, so we insured my life for another ten thousand dollars. This policy allowed funds to build into the policy value. We also insured the mortgage on our house. There were other minor revisions to our finances.

We packed our furniture and belongings and had them shipped to Salinas. Living in government housing means that someone will come and inspect the apartment so everything must be cleaned. Our next door neighbors allowed us to stay at their apartment for a couple of days until we cleared our quarters. By the time everything was done and we had clearance to depart, it was late in the afternoon and was beginning to snow. Our neighbors wanted us to stay until morning, however we wanted to leave. I remember that when we arrived at the Colorado /New Mexico border we stopped the car and we all exited the car and said, "Hooray!, Hooray!, we are finally our of Colorado". We then started to look for shelter for the night. We had notified the people who were renting our house that we were coming home so they had already moved by the time we arrived home. We did not have keys to our house and although there were keys next door at Syl and Lorraine's house, they were not home so we had to break a window to get inside. I spent my leave time getting the family settled, our children into school and before I knew it, it was time for my departure.

Chapter 10

MY TOUR IN VIETNAM

I stayed at home until the very last minute before going to Oakland to report for duty and to be processed for overseas duty. I had been there for about two days before the weekend when Syl, Lorraine and my wife came to visit me. It seemed that my babe had received a letter from the Internal Revenue Service because I had neglected to complete page 2 of our return. She was afraid of the IRS's threat. She did not know that they could not do anything to me because I would by then be in Vietnam where the filing of taxes is not required. On the other hand I was always very glad to see her one more time, so I completed the form and mailed it back to them. If I had not done this, my honey would have worried needlessly. The next day I was among a group that departed on a new airplane, its maiden voyage. I did not know it then, but riding on a new plane can be troublesome. We took off at night and after flying all night, we arrived at Midway. The pilot announced that we were landing at Midway. Looking out the side of the plane, I could not see an island, only water; even when we were very close to the ground I still could not see an island. The wheels finally touched down on dry land. After refueling, we were ready to take off again. Half of the airplane was extending over the water as it took every inch of runway to get off the ground again. Needless to say we made it and we continued on toward Vietnam. Then the pilot announced that one—half of the instrument panel had gone out and we would have to land in the Philippians. We stayed overnight cramped up in tiny accommodations. When the plane was repaired, we took off again and this time we made it to Vietnam, however we could not land immediately because the airbase was under attack. We circled around until the all clear signal was given. The pilot made a swift landing and hurried us off the plane and he and the crew took off again.

I did not immediately go to my unit, the 4th Infantry Division because after reviewing my records, the replacement personnel wanted to keep me there, I had to wait for the decision to be made. I stayed there a few more days before it was decided that I must go north to my duty assignment. That night we boarded a C-130 aircraft enroute to Pleiku Air Base and then on to Camp Inari, the home of the 4th Infantry Division. When I arrived, I was assigned to the Division Personnel Management headed by Master Sergeant Caniff. It took me a couple of days to see what my new troops were doing. My quarters were in the senior NCO hut where I roomed with anther Sergeant First Class named Lounsbury. It was not long before I knew that I had to make some changes because everyone was working too hard for their output.

The first thing that I noticed was a line of soldiers outside of our office. Upon inquiring what the soldiers wanted, I learned that they were being given their assignment after completing their Vietnam tour. I asked the clerk if we only one copy of the received the assignment roster and found that we received six copies. It was during the morning that I made this inquiry, so I told my clerk to continue until noon at which time we took three of our copies with a cover letter of instructions to the battalions to give the assignments to their men. No more long lines and everyone received their assignments faster.

I was called to the Adjutant General's office one morning. All of the officers and senior NCO's were there, with smiles on their faces. Normally such a meeting means either someone is in trouble or something good is about to happen. It was then that I learned that I had been awarded the Army Commendation Medal for my work at Fort Carson, Colorado. This is the second time that I have been awarded this medal. Here in Vietnam we do not have time for a parade so the medal is just given in the setting I just described. In my letter to my dear wife, I had something else besides the war to tell her.

I had been in Vietnam for a couple of months now and began to notice the makeup of the division. I noticed that some of the components were of not much use like the two tank battalions because the fighting was mostly in something called a fire base. However the helicopters were widely used so additional aviation units were obtained from the 1st Aviation Brigade. This type of warfare seemed familiar to me and I soon realized that when I was serving in France, I worked on a project called TASTA-70; when I was first appointed an action officer. There was other like units serving here that were also a part of that project. This was the first time that I had actually seen some of my ideas put into practice on such a wide scale.

Master sergeant Caniff had rotated home and I was now the senior NCO of the Management Branch. The division has a policy that the senior NCO must live with his troops. When I saw his room, I did not like it, so I obtained some plywood and lumber and began to reconstruct it as I wanted. This later in my tour proved to be my downfall though I did know it then. I put all my carpentry skills to work and made my room very neat. I even had wall plugs for my television, air condition unit and my refrigerator. I obtained some green paint and painted the inside. Some civilian workers that generated the electricity for the camp lived across the road from us. I got to know them very well and always traded things that they could not get for things that I could get easily. When they had liver and onions for dinner, I was always their guest. This is because our liver and onions tasted like shoe leather and theirs were tender and juicy. At home in Salinas, my wife would never cook liver or anything that comes from the inside of an animal.

One day during the noon hour a group of us were behind the senior NCO hut cooking steaks on the bar-be-cue pit because we probably did not like what was being served in the mess hall. As we were eating our food two military police came by and said they were going to check the village that was situated just outside the camp. We all talked there for a while and I jumped into the jeep and said that I had never visited the village and wanted to see what it was like. Just before we took off, one of my troops reminded me that I had promised to talk to a soldier about his problem immediately after lunch. I then jumped out of the jeep and told the police that I would ride with them another day. They drove off out toward the village and as they cleared the gate, they were ambushed and both were killed. If I had gone with them, I would have been killed also. I guess God was looking over me.

Everything seemed to be running smoothly when I noticed another of my troops working much harder than the others. Being a good leader, I went to him to determine why he had to work so hard, especially during the beginning of the month. It seems that we were required to make a report to higher headquarters listing all personnel, officers and enlisted that extended their tour in Vietnam. During this period we had draftees in the army and if they extended for a period of three months, they could go home and be discharged instead of being reassigned to a stateside post and completing their full two years. This report had to be typed alphabetically by rank, by the number of months extended. All during the month he approved these applications and had a card that he prepared to keep track of approvals. Only after the first of the month did his workload increase. Again, I told him that I could do nothing for the current month, but beginning next month I would streamline his workload. I told him that when he prepared the card on approval, he was to collect them until he had about fifty, and then give them to me in batches of fifty until the end of the month. I took the cards to the Data Processing Branch and had one of the clerks to punch the cards in a format that I found in the circular that required the report. I then wrote a list program so that at the end of the month, all that was necessary was to punch the last batch of cards, sort them in the proper order and run my list program. He was so surprised that he did not have to spend hours, some at night, typing the report. When we submitted this report to higher headquarters, I soon got a call asking if I still had the cards that made our report and when I said that I had, they requested them in order to save them work. I also told them that I had used the record layout that was in the circular so that reformatting the cards was not necessary. It was not long before the circular was changed to require larger units with data processing capability to prepare the cards instead of a written report.

In one of my letters from Nobi she told me that our children were playing in the family room and that our daughter Eva had accidently kicked the glass door leading outside onto the patio and that the door broke and cut her leg very badly. While she took Eva to the hospital at Fort Ord, our neighbor Syl came over, measured and purchased another glass and repaired the door before Nobi returned home. All she had to pay for was the new piece of glass. I was so gratifying to have such neighbors especially since I had to be away so often.

I next noticed that another clerk who processed those completing their Vietnam tour had a list of the personnel who were to ship on a particular day. The last three entries were lined out and three new names added. I did not think too much of this the first time I saw it because errors happen and this could very well have been an error that was corrected. The next day when this happened, I became suspicious so I began to look to see if this was occurring daily. Having ascertained that it was a daily occurrence, I asked the clerk about it and was told that the sergeant in Records Branch had taken the men off. I knew that this was improper so I told my clerk that I would accompany him the next morning as he prepared to ship those eligible to go home. Sure enough the sergeant from Records Branch attempted to do the same only this time I introduced myself to him and stopped him from changing the shipment roster. The three new entries to the roster immediately spoke up and said that they had paid the sergeant fifty dollars per day that they were going home early for a total of $350.00 per person or $1050.00 for changing the three troops. Having heard this I told my clerk to ship the original entries to the roster. The new entries plus the sergeant were told to come to the Adjutant General's office to make statements because I was going to see that this sergeant was punished. On the way, the sergeant asked if he could go into his office and get something to defend his actions. I have to admit that I was naïve as to where someone could go in Vietnam. We waited, and waited for him to show up only to find that he did have an out for himself, because we were told that he had been medical evacuated from the country. I never found out how many others were involved in this scheme to fleece the field troops, but I did put a stop to it. I told my clerk that I could not do too much to change the system because it was in the middle of the month, but by the beginning of the next month I would have a much better system in place. I had Data Processing training during my tour in France so I was familiar with computers and had a working relation with the Data Processing Branch of the division. We received the transportation in bulk, so it was up to us to determine the names of each person on each flight to the United States. I wrote a program that checked every criterion for redeployment home and tested it thoroughly. Afterwards each month we just screened the computer records for everyone eligible to return home each month. Now no one could change the daily shipment, but me, so we were pretty sure that there would not be any more fraud. One month the Chief of Staff of the Division and the Commander of Support Command came to the office and asked for me by name as there were questions as to whether it was the proper time for the Commander of Supply and Transport battalion was being redeployed at the proper time. They believed that this commander had pressured us to move up his time to be shipped home. When I assured them that this was not the case, they asked me how we made the shipment roster.

I explained that we produced a program that checked every criterion in the regulations governing departure from the country and that we screened the computer records for the deployment date and when the program was run, it made the roster. At that time we had cards for records. The Chief of Staff asked me if he dropped the records would it make an exact copy of the shipment roster. I assured him that it would and after having another clerk sort the cards in the proper order and running the program again, it did name an exact copy of the shipment. He then told me that our system was the fairest that he had seen in Vietnam and went to II Field Forces Headquarters and bragged about it and I had to give my program to the other two divisions there. This is the second time that my innovations to improve my operations were used to improve others throughout the command.

A soldier came to me one day and told me that he had made application to return to Germany after his tour in Vietnam was completed and that the application had not been approved. He stated that he wanted to return to Germany because his wife, a German national, was not permitted to immigrate to the United States because she had a spot on her lungs and that the State Department required more time to evaluate the spot. He also told me that he had requested reconsideration of his request and that the reconsideration report had also not been approved. I saw myself in this soldier's dilemma because when we were in Germany my wife had to apply for an exit/entry permit and she also had a spot on her lungs but her permit was approved because there was additional data in her file to determine that the spot had remained the same size. I have always been one to obey all regulations but in this case I could see no reason to send this man to the United States when his wife and children were stuck in Germany just because some regulation said so. There were soldiers being sent to Germany from Vietnam, so when this man's time was up, I just changed the control number and issued orders sending him to Germany. As I write this, it has been more than forty years since I broke this army rule so I guess it is too late for me to be disciplined for it.

Every now and then the enemy would let us know they were still there by attacking the camp with rockets. The First Sergeant had told us many times that the sand bags providing protection around the doors of our hut were not high enough. Since only senior NCO personnel lived in our hut the First Sergeant did not see fit to detail someone in charge of completing this task and no one did. Lounsbury and I had a system of stacking our clothes on top of our flak jacket, followed by our helmet. Our rifles were hung by the door. This system allowed us to get out of the room quickly with all of our gear. One night when we were undergoing a rocket attack Lounsbury somehow beat me out of the room. As we were running down the hall, a piece of shrapnel came over the opening by the door and stuck in the floor between Lounsbury's legs. Because I was right behind him, I could see the little brown spot come onto his white shorts. I know this was not funny, but I could not stop laughing even after we were in the bunker. Everyone there wanted to know what I was laughing about but because I wanted to stay friends with him, I would not say. Needless to say, the sandbags around the doors had several new layers immediately after the "all clear" signal was given.

We had been having rocket attacks almost every night, in spite of constant shelling from several large 155mm Howitzers placed on a hill near the center of the camp. To combat this, we were all ordered to form a large circle around the camp and moved forward from there for a distance of four to five miles looking for and destroying anything that looked like places from which the rockets were launched. Senior NCOs were to keep the troops moving in a straight line and not bunched up. When we were about four miles out while I was watching my troops keeping then on course, I was not looking where I was going and stepped into a trap, which was a large hole dug about five feet into the ground with sharpened bamboo sticks that had been dipped into some type of poison, I was lucky that I stepped on the edge of the pit and did not fall to the bottom. Instead I sprained my left leg. We kept going a little further before we stopped for lunch. After lunch my leg stiffened on me so that I could hardly walk. I tried to walk because we were returning to camp but the pain became so intense that I had to stop. The medics came and accessed my situation and called for a helicopter to come pick me up. I waited there with two medics who were left for my aid but before the helicopter came another younger soldier was brought to my position who had received a much more serious wound. It appeared that he had been shot and was bleeding badly. When the helicopter did arrive, there was only room for one of us. Being the leader that I was, I told the medics to put the wounded soldier on the helicopter and I would wait until it came back for me. Unfortunately for me, I learned that the helicopter was not permitted to return to the field therefore the two medics and I had to hike back regardless of my leg. As we trudged back we came upon a creek that had been filled with water on our outbound trip but was now dry. We gingerly worked our way down one side and when going up the other side, my leg hurt so bad that I could not make it without help. One of the medics came down to help me get up, the other medic asked me to throw up my rifle because it was in the way. As he tried to catch my rifle, it came down in such a way that it busted his hand. Now we had to stop and bandage his hand. By the time we arrived at the starting point I instructed the two medics to take any vehicle that they saw and we rode the rest of the way. I know that I should have gone to get medical attention but was so angry that I just wanted to go and lie down. I avowed never to go on any more of these games, and never did.

My sweetheart and I continued our daily letter writing routine like we always did when I had to leave the family. Even when there was no time to write, we would write "I LOVE YOU' on a piece of paper and mail it. One afternoon when I was reading my letter I must have been talking out loud as Lounsbury asked me what I said. I told him that my wife had accepted a job at the school near our home. He asked me if my wife had asked my permission before accepting the job. I told him that my wife was not required to ask my permission before doing anything she wanted to do. She is my partner, not my servant I continued. I continued reading my letter in silence and learned that she had been helping my younger daughter's teacher in the classroom and because she was there so often, she was encouraged to take the job that had become open. I was happy that she was doing something besides staying home as our children were growing up, and we could always use the extra money.

Until now, everything I have written about the army life in Vietnam was about the Redeployment unit of personnel management. Now that master sergeant Caniff had departed and I was in charge, I began to notice the Classification and Assignment unit of my branch. I learned that the Commanding General required from us a report of the fighting strength of each unit in the division. No army report is made with this information; therefore we had to manually count only the combat personnel omitting the support personnel. This proved to be another use for the computers next door. Since that report would be made after the casualty report was run at midnight, the data processing personnel would not take on this added responsibility and since I was the only outside person qualified to operate the machine I was the one to make the report. This was not a hard task but lengthy. In order to obtain that necessary data, fifteen trays of cards would be processed taking about two hours. I would then leave the raw data listing on my sergeant's desk who would rearrange the data on one sheet of paper for the general.

Rumors were flying about that we were going to get a larger allocations for promotion soon so everyone was trying to spruce up their records, especially those that would count for promotion. One thing that would give points toward promotion was medals awarded. One cheap way to be awarded medals was by the award of the Air Medal. All that was required was for one to sign on as a crew member on combat missions six times. All combat missions did not always mean coming in contact with the enemy, some missions only required riding around on a helicopter. I decided that I could use a few points so I put my name on the already long list. When my name came to the top, I received my instructions and mounted the helicopter. At first we were just going around the camp and the town, but before we returned, a real combat mission was called and we joined several other helicopters and went to help some ground troops in trouble. I actually had to fire my machine gun. When we returned to base I was so glad that I did not have to do this on a daily basis. I never signed on as a crew again and did not get my Air Medal.

The love of my life wrote to me that my son, James, had gotten a newspaper route and worked very hard delivering the morning paper every day. Unfortunately for him, many of his customers would not pay him for their papers, so he quit the route and kept all of the money for himself. She told me that she had paid the bill herself when the newspaper company complained that they had not been paid. I wrote him a letter telling him that what he did was not honest business practices although he did deserve the money; the company also acted in good faith and deserved their share of the money also. I commended him for his desire to work and for doing a good job in the process. But he always must do the right thing.

The rumors approved to be correct. We did get some promotion allocations, quite a bit of them. In the headquarters we could keep two to the grade of master sergeant. Of the two one was allotted to the Adjutant General's office. The two leading candidates for this promotion was between one other that worked in the Adjutant General's office proper and myself who worked in Personnel Management. Only the records were considered and I was beat out by one point. I was not only disappointed but thought I should have gotten it because I had done so many more things to improve the command and one that improved conditions for all Army units in Vietnam. The ruling of a major point went against me. This had to do with proficiency test scores. I was able to take my test before leaving my previous duty station and was in the top ten percent and was being paid proficiency pay. The other candidate did not take the test although he could have but didn't. The score for those not taking the test was more generous than for those who took the test, therefore I lost. This hurt me very much and there would be no more promotions to the grade of Master Sergeant in the field. All future promotions to this grade or higher would be made in Washington D.C.

My tour in Vietnam was getting short and my thoughts were on returning home to see my family and the love of my life. Some replacements were being assigned to the various combat units of the division when into the office came my old friend Porterfield whom I served with in France. I was so happy to see him that I disrupted his processing and took him to talk over old timers.

Since I did not get the promotion, I was determined to get something out of being in Vietnam. I came up with a plan that would permit me to go to Japan for a few days without it costing any money or leave time. The NCO in charge of the post office agreed to test my theory and wanted to know what would happen if someone caught on to the scheme. I told him that since he had authorization in the form of travel tickets the only thing he could be charged with is two or three days leave. He stated that he had plenty of leave so when it was time for him to leave, he was given travel tickets from Vietnam to Japan, and from Japan to California. When he arrived at his home port, he wrote us back and said that it worked like a charm. I set myself up to do the same thing. After my arrival in Japan I would look up some of the people we knew and some of Nobi's family. Of course I never had the chance to do any of it because a few days before I was to leave, I had the worst accident of my life.

Chapter 11

THE MEDICAL EVACUATION CHAIN

My tour in Vietnam was now down to about two weeks when some of my troops came to me and told me that some of the Vietnamese workers were spraying the perimeter fence and that the wind had blown some of the spray into our hut. I instructed them to get some electric fans and start at one of the hut and blow the mist out and that no one was to sleep with his head toward the walls because some of the mist may be trapped there. I then went to perform my night duty at the data processing branch. I returned to my room about three o'clock in the morning and forgot all about the spray. I had not done anything about getting the mist from my room and was going to sleep in the bed of anyone that was on guard for the night. I was so tired that I went directly to my room and went to sleep in my own bed. The next morning I could not hold my body upright as I was so weak. I cannot remember whether I went to breakfast or not but I do remember that the early morning sun felt good on my skin; therefore I went to my office that faced the east and into the sun. I remember that I had to lean against the wall to hold myself upright. I guess that I was lucky that some medic friends came to ask a favor of me early that morning because when they saw the condition I was in, they told me I should see the doctor. I said that I had too much work to do and could not spare the time waiting for the doctor. They said that they would see that I was the next patient once we were at the dispensary. They half carried me and true to their word, I was the next patient to see the doctor.

The doctor thought that I was having a heart attack and administered nitroglycerin that did not help. He instructed me to have a complete physical examination to determine what was wrong. I got up to leave but my body gave way and I collapsed onto the floor and lost all sense of conscience. Our camp was south of the city of Pleiku about three miles out of town. Then comes the city and to the north lies the Airbase and garrison which contained the hospital. It was about nine o'clock in the morning when I was examined by the doctor. When I gained my sense of conscience I was in the intensive care ward of the hospital and it was late in the afternoon. I was also hooked up to several medical machines and/or pumps. I had no idea how or when I had been taken there. I asked the nurse where I was and was told immediately to be quiet and not talk because I was very sick. It was not until one of sergeants came to visit me that I learned that the medic friends had returned to my office and asked my troops about any unusual occurrences that would cause me to become sick and was told about the spray which turned out to be Agent Orange that was supposed to have been destroyed and not used any longer.

When I had been in the hospital for seven days without much improvement, the doctor came to me and told me he had a problem that needed my consent. He told me that I could not remain in there in the hospital because it was an Evacuation Hospital and I either had to return to duty or be evacuated to another hospital out of the country. He also said that I could not be evacuated while in the intensive care unit. I told him to do whatever he must do, so to solve his problem I was transferred to a general ward for a few hours and would be evacuated to Japan. The night I was to be put aboard the airplane, we had another rocket attack and had to wait until it was over. During the attack they put us under our beds because there were no bunkers for the hospital. When the attack was over, they started putting us on board the aircraft. My "medevac" tag indicated that I had to be suspended in the air not placed near the bulkheads of the aircraft because the doctors were afraid that the vibration would harm me. When my turn came to be placed on board, the orderly did not read my tag and thought that he was doing me a favor by placing me where there was more space; however this was next to a bulkhead. I brought this to the attention of the sergeant in charge of loading the aircraft and he said that I would be taken off the aircraft and would have to go the next day. Before I could be moved the pilot closed the large doors of the aircraft so nothing could be changed. The sergeant brought my several pillows and placed them between me and the bulkhead. The doctor came and gave me a shot of something that knocked me out so I have no knowledge of the aircraft ever leaving the ground. The next thing that I knew was the aircraft landing at Yokota Air Force Base in Japan. What came to my mind then was that Nobi and I used to live in a small town that lies at the end of this same runway. We were all put aboard ambulances and transported to the hospital where we would remain for another seven days.

After two or three days in this hospital, I began to feel better but I was still weak. I now began to notice the food that was being served to me. Prior to this time I had not eaten anything. I noticed that my food always had a silver cover but under this cover one could not recognize the contents as being food. Seems as though the cook was angry with my food. It was so dry and listless that it could not be recognized as food. Of course I did not eat it. The only food that I had was some ice cream that the orderly slipped to me after the nurses had gone. Another sergeant that was about my age was also in the same ward. Something was wrong with his stomach so his food was boiled. Just for fun, I would get into my wheel chair, go over to his bed and tell him to squish it up into tube like and flush it down the toilet in order to cut out the middle man. I would then go back to my bed. Although I was weak, overall I did feel better. The sergeant in charge of the personnel office was a sergeant first class that I had known at Fort Ord. I asked the ward orderly to take me to the hospital headquarters so that I could see my old friend. I stayed at the headquarters building for about an hour but on the way back the orderly and I went to the Post Exchange and hung around looking at things we had no intention of buying. When we got back to our hospital ward, the chief nurse was very angry with both of us. The orderly took most of the dressing down and was told that I was a patient and had no authority there. She also informed us that I had missed the times for the taking of three medicines.

My seven days here at the hospital in Japan were almost up. When my doctor visited me that day, he told me that I either had to return to duty or be transferred to the States. Being flip as I sometimes am, I asked the doctor if I was being returned to duty. What he told me next brought me down to earth. He told me that he wanted me to go before a medical board which would have retired me from active service with a disability of at least seventy-five percent. I was not ready to leave the service so I told him that I was going to get better and that I had many more years to serve. He then told me that I should be dead and that I was never going to get better than I am now. He left by asking me to think about going before the medical board, but no one could make me do it. I knew that it was God's will that I survived the amount of time that I spent breathing Agent Orange vapors.

Two days later several of us were put aboard ambulances and transported to Yokota Air Force Base to await further transportation home. I was able to look out and see the many things as we passed along the streets. When I passed along these same streets enroute to the hospital I was in no condition to enjoy the scenery. Upon arrival at the Hospital Transfer Station I had a nice bed that overlooked the working of the airbase. I could see planes taking off and landings and people working etc. I had a pretty little red headed nurse who was about twenty-two years old. She was really something to look at. I asked her if I could get into my wheel chair and push myself over by a large window that almost covered the wall. She gave her permission as long as I remained in the wheel chair. I had been watching the activity of the air base for about most of an hour when a very large airplane carrying wounded soldiers arrived. Upon examining these soldiers, I could see that they were from the 4th Division that I had been assigned. Some of these soldiers were still in battlefield gear and their wounds were still dressed with battlefield bandages. This means that they had not had any professional medical care and was brought here directly from the battlefield. I do not know what motivated me to do what I did, but I got up from my wheel chair and began helping to put these guys into beds. I knew from my own experience how the system worked so I had no trouble determining where each person was to go. I selected those that had the use of both hands and arms because they had to help me get them into the bed. I helped get the whole plane unloaded and was standing with the group folding blankets. I felt no discomfort while working. As we were there talking, my nurse happened to pass by and asked me what I was doing. Before I could answer, the person in charge of the detail asked, "Wasn't he sent out here to help us". She told her no, that I belong in that wheel chair over by the window; she then looked at me and told me to get to my wheel chair. I took a few steps and collapsed into unconsciousness.

There was no doctor present because the day was Sunday and they were not expecting the new troops that had just come in. Now they had to get a doctor from someplace nearby or from the golf course. I do not know how long I was out this time but when I did gain conscience, the doctor was hovering over me very angry. He told me that if as much as raise my arms above my head; they would convene a court-martial at my bed and asked if I understood. I asked him, "What if I want to read". He said for me to get a candy striper to hold my book. After examining me again, he left. The next day all of us that were enroute to the States were put aboard a huge C5A aircraft. Those of us who had to remain on our stretchers were in one place while others had seats for the long trip over the ocean. This time there was no mistake as where to put me as I was suspended into a stack with three others. After the airplane was in the air, I, along with two others was given an injection that made us go right to sleep. Most of the trip to Travis Air Force Base in California I did not remember, but when I came out of my stupor we were landing. I, along with others going to Fort Ord Hospital was put aboard a much smaller aircraft that landed in Monterey. From there we went by ambulance to Fort Ord.

Because I was still classified as being very sick, I was put in a ward that had many older people who were on their last leg of life. I did not see any nurses or doctors in this ward, only one middle aged sergeant. I asked him where the telephone was because I wanted to notify my wife that I was here at Fort Ord. He told me that I could not get out of bed to use a telephone and that I could not have visitors. I then told him that unless he stayed and watched me, I was going to find a phone. He then told me that he was going to get a doctor to have me transferred to another ward, which was alright with me. My new ward had many young soldiers in it and was a very lively place. I soon found a telephone and called the love of my life. I also had turned on my charm and had gotten the new doctor to let me go home; however this doctor wanted to talk with Nobi first. When she arrived, and came running into my arms, she was the most beautiful sight that I had seen for over a year. She was so pretty that I just held her in my arms and kissed her so hard on the mouth that I almost passed out. As a rule she does not like to display this type of emotion in public. I took her by the hand and led her to the doctor so that we could be on our way home.

The doctor took her into his office while I had to stay by my bed and was not allowed to hear their discussion. After they had finished their talk and Nobi came to my bed, she seemed a whole lot different and she would not touch me when I tried to hold her hand. We went to the car and started home. Again I tried to touch her on the leg but she removed my hand by gently slapping it. I was really puzzled now and wondered what the doctor had told her. I knew that I had not done anything like messing around but I just could not understand what had come over her. The children were all at school and we had the house to ourselves, so I wanted to go to bed but she would not. I asked her what was the matter and was told nothing was wrong and that I should go to my easy chair and rest. I went and sat in my chair and when she passed close by, I pulled her down into my lap only for her to get right up and go into the kitchen. I really did not understand what was going on and she would not tell me. Night finally came and we went to bed. She stayed on her side of the bed without even letting our hands touch. I could not stand it any longer and in a firm tone ask her to tell me what the doctor had told her. She took a deep breath and told me that the doctor had told her that she was not to get me excited in any way or to exert myself too much. We were not to have intercourse until I was much stronger. Any of these things would kill me. I said that was silly and that I was stronger than the doctor gave me credit for. Anything I said did not cut any ice with her; however she did tell me that she wanted to make love as much as I did and we would suffer together. Needless to say I spent another night almost alone in my bed.

I was required to be near my bed at 6 o'clock in the morning when the doctor made his rounds. I was not allowed to drive so Nobi had to drive me to camp. The next morning when the doctor came around, he just looked at me and knowingly smiled as he examined me. This went on for about a week being able to look at my sweetheart and not being able to touch her seemed to me was doing me more harm. The next morning when the doctor examined me, I told him so. He gave us permission to have light petting but still no intercourse or heavy petting. He said that if my blood pressure did rise, I might lose conscience and would need medical attention immediately; so no heavy petting or I could not go home. That night all I was permitted to do was that she would lie in my arms until she went to sleep. I know that my wife loved me and I loved her. She was my whole world and because of this, I could stand this treatment.

I had been making my daily trips to the hospital in the early morning and returning home after being examined by the doctor for two months when I received information that the Department of the Army had announced in a circular all eligible persons for promotion to the grade of Master Sergeant and that my name was on it. Now I had to jockey myself to duty because being in the medical evacuation chain might keep my promotion from being announced. I began working on the doctor that day. I also knew that he would not let me go to duty if I could not even make love to my lovely wife. That same night when we went to bed I started kissing her and caressing her where I knew would get her worked up. At first she told me to stop or I would hurt myself but I just kept it up until she gave in and told me "OK, but take it easy". The next day when I was being examined by the doctor, he looked into my face and said, "You have had intercourse". "Take it easy from now on; let her do most of the work". Now all that I had to do was make him believe that I was strong enough to go to duty. I kept asking every day if I could go to duty and one day, I guess to shut me up, he told me that I could. The next day I received my orders assigning me with the Experimental Troops of Combat Development Command, Experimentation Center at Fort Ord.

Chapter 12

MY SECOND TOUR AT FORT ORD

The next day I reported for duty and was assigned a job as Personnel Staff NCO. This is not a hard job so I was sure that I would have no trouble fulfilling my duties. I had been there for about a month when a notice was posted that the entire unit would go to Hunter Liggett Military Reservation, training ground about fifty miles south of Fort Ord. I went to the supply room to get my gear. The supply sergeant told me that he could not issue me anything because I was not going on the trip. I became very angry. This was the first sign that the Agent Orange had damaged my brain because I never liked field training anyway and normally would be delighted to not go. The anger made me lose rationality, so I went storming in to see the first sergeant who calmed me down a little and then said to me, "I did not want to tell you this now, but since you pushed the issue, you are being transferred to the post". He continued, "Just look at you, you can hardly stand up. We need able bodied people in this unit because the training is tough, I am sorry". A few days letter I had orders assigning me to the post, where I was assigned to the Personnel Division, with enlisted records.

The building that housed the Enlisted Records Branch was converted from a barrack that housed troops. There were civilian personnel as well as military personnel; both women and men. I did not have an officer in charge so my immediate supervisor was the Chief, Personnel Division. I was blessed with a secretary to type my correspondence. I went around and got acquainted with all of my staff. I remember one civilian lady whose name was Ester Lopez, a large woman that outweighed me by at least 50 pounds. She had an opinion on everything and I knew that we were not going to get along very well. She had been at her job for several years and I have to admit knew her job well. One of her faults was that she had to have the last word on everything and that is my job.

I remembered that the doctor had told me that I would not get any better than I was now; and the words of the first sergeant from the experimental troops still stung, so I decided to prove them wrong. I started going to the gym every day at noon in an attempt to rebuild my body. The first day I could only walk the length of the gym before being exhausted, but I stuck to it. The next week I was able to add the width of the gym to the length, meaning I could walk around half of the gym. By the end of the first month I could do five laps around the gym. My progress was slow but I was determined. Also at home my lovely wife too was remembering what the doctor had told her so our love making was much less often than before I went to Vietnam. If I had not known that she loved me, I might have been angry. I knew that she was trying to make sure that I would survive. I also remembered that she told me before I left for Vietnam to come back to her even if I did not have arms or legs. With these things in mind, I just took whatever she felt comfortable with giving. Sometimes it would only be holding her hand; others times I could go as far as getting a lengthy kiss before she made me stop. I continued going to the gym and building my body until I could make at least ten laps around the gym by running instead of just walking. It was time that I took my body building outside, so I used the layout of the area to mark off about the distance of a track used for track and field exercises and alternately walked and ran around this area. Now that I had proved the doctor wrong, I began to find excuses not to do my daily exercises until I had stopped doing them altogether.

One day immediately after lunch while in the office, one of my young soldiers came up to me and asked if I had missed him. When I told that that I had not, he told me that he had been absent without leave (AWOL). Well he had not officially been AWOL because that requires being gone for more than 24 hours and he had been working part of the morning. I asked him what his trouble was and he told that me that he had some pressing personal business back home, just outside of Chicago, Ill. That had to be taken care of and that he had thought of just going without saying anything to anyone. His military training made him return and get help which was why he had returned. This took place on a Thursday afternoon, much too early to give him a three day pass, and he did not have leave time. I called up the first sergeant and brought him up to date on the young soldiers troubles and asked him if we could bend the rules just a bit by letting him leave now, and I would assure him that some of my troops would come up and sign him out on Friday making the three day pass legal. The next thing was to call over to the Naval Air Station at Monterey and asked if they had any flights that were going in the vicinity of Chicago and was told that such a plane was getting ready to warm up for that destination and if we had a passenger for it, he had to get there within the next thirty minutes. I told my young soldier than I expected him to be standing at my desk when I arrived at work on Monday morning. I then had someone to drive him to Monterey. This scheme worked well and he was signed out on time, satisfying the first sergeant. On Monday morning my young soldier was standing at my desk smiling. He said to me that he had no idea that he could get the kind of help we gave to him. He turned out to be one of my best soldiers as well as a very good clerk.

My children are growing up now and will soon want to leave home to make a life for themselves. James is in his last year of high school and is concentrating on his track and field events. He knows that he is too small to play college football. When Nobi and I go to his meets, his coach complains that he does just enough to win and is not doing his best. The coach says that when he calls him on it, James tells him that, "I won, didn't I". I told the coach not to waste time when he gets the "Mr. Spock" attitude because when he was small, one Christmas I tried to make him eat eggs that was served him for breakfast by not letting him get up from the table until he had eaten his breakfast. Although it was Christmas, he sat at the table all day. My Eva was noticing boys and there were a few hanging around our house.

During this time, one of Nobi's friends by the name of Yoshi Carter, had gotten a divorce from Carter and had married a man named Hill. Our friendship with Yoshie had been cultivated from the time we were living in Ord Village when we first came to Fort Ord. They had been the best of friends for a long time. We did not want her to marry Hill, but I guess that being lonely and raising two boys alone, she needed a mate. Yoshie and Hill had had a daughter who name was Louise, but we all called her Lulu. As time passed, Hill began to show his true self and began teasing the boys about their father. To us, this was cruel because children are never responsible for the things their parents do. In addition to being cruel to her boys, he did not treat Yoshie very well either therefore they soon divorced. Hill was very angry and spiteful because of this, and would not sign a request for an Army Identification Card for his young daughter because he thought that in some way, it would aid Yoshie. Yoshie came to visit Nobi and somewhere in their conversation, she made this known to my sweetheart. Nobi asked me if there was something that I could do for her, so I told Yoshie to come and see me at my office the next morning. I had been given permission to approve and sign these requests in the performance of my duties in that an officer was not assigned to my branch. I knew that since the sponsor would not sign the request, I should have sent the request for determination to the Army Finance and Accounting Office at Indianapolis, Indiana, but I knew that Lulu needed medical attention immediately and that sending the request away, would delay her getting medical attention. Also our friendship clouded my judgment so I approved her request. Hill was furious with this and tried to make trouble for me. He went directly to the Adjutant General with his complaint, who called me to his office. When I told him the complete story and that his records indicated that he was being paid an allowance for dependents, this action was justified. Yoshie was allowed to keep the card, however my authority to approve these requests was withdrawn. I was told then that the withdrawal was not due to my judgment, but he thought that I should send these requests to the Identification Branch who did have an officer assigned.

At work a few military police were hanging around my office trying to make time with the women soldiers that I had working in my office. I have to admit that some of them were very good looking and one or two could be called beautiful. I let the boys know that they could come around during the noon hour but I did not want them interrupting their work. Our Sergeant Major convinced the Adjutant General that the senior NCOs should get together at the club every Friday afternoon to get a better understanding of each other's work and problems. This turned out to be nothing more than a drinking session as little or no work was ever discussed. One Friday I was very busy and did not attend. About an hour later I was called by the

Adjutant General to get my butt up to the club for our meeting. I was angry, but I went and never missed another so called meeting. At one of these meetings that lasted long after duty hours several of us were very drunk. As I was driving home, I guess I must have been weaving over the road and was stopped by the military police. I was lucky because these were the same boys that were hanging about my office. They offered to take me home but I told them that my car knew the way. They just said, "Take it easy going home".

The promotion list came out from Washington DC of the persons to be promoted to the grades of Master Sergeant and Sergeant Major. This list was named "Recommended List". My name was number 371 on the list so I could count on my promotion being announced in about three months. It was about this same time that the command had been notified that I had been awarded the Bronze Star Medal for my work in Vietnam. All senior NCOs gathered in the Adjutant General's office to hear the citation read and the awarding of the medal. A week later I was moved to Personnel Management Branch and the sergeant there took charge in Enlisted Records Branch.

I was not at my new assignment long before I noticed that the officer in charge, Captain Carcuff, was cool to me. I did not know what I was doing that did not satisfy him, nor would he come right out and tell me that I was doing something that he did not like. It was at this time that I made the acquaintance of Chief Warrant Officer Frank Myers. We became friends that lasted many years after we no longer served in the Army. I asked Frank what the Captain had against me. He told me that when I wrote memorandums or any correspondence to the command group or to the senior staff, the typist wrote my name as writer. The captain wanted credit for this writing, so I instructed the typist to put the captain's name as the writer. From that time, the Captain and I got along very well.

Eva and Robert are now attending Salinas High School and James is going to Hartnell College. Because of the bus schedule it is necessary for them to get a car of their own. Both have their driver's license. Nobi and I bought them a used brown Chevrolet 2-door sedan, vintage mid-sixties that they named "Leroy". They were only supposed to drive it to school and back home, but according to the gas usage, it went everywhere. James was too small for college football, so he concentrated on his track and field events. Robert played both football and ran track. Whenever Robert was the daily driver of Leroy, he would drive through the alley behind Packwood's Furniture store. This angered Mister Packwood so much that he complained to me, so I asked Robert to use another shortcut to Main Street. Most of the time all I had to do was ask my children to do things and they would obey. Robert did obey and we had no more trouble with Mister Packwood.

On one occasion both Eva and Robert was hospitalized at Fort Ord for minor surgery. Eva had tonsil trouble and Robert had his appendix removed. It was during this time that Eva was also diagnosed with a disease called Lupus. There was not too much known about this disease at the time. One thing known was that she could not stay in the sunlight very long. She was referred to a Doctor Anthony Smith here in Salinas who was supposed to be the residence expert. He was a very fine doctor and he gave her good treatment for her illness. From the beginning he informed her that there was no cure for her disease and that the disease would only get worse. He also told her that during the later stages, the pain would be so intense the medicine would do very little good. This information was very hard for us to take, but we are a close family and all would pull together to see this through.

Every year the military required that we undergo a proficiency test. The test booklets are in the care of the branch where I am the senior NCO. Although we have officers in the branch, the NCOs are the ones who are responsible. One Saturday afternoon Frank Myers came to my home and told me that an inventory of the test booklets had been done and that one test was missing. This would not ordinarily cause too much concern except that the missing test was one that is given to all of us who work in my branch as well as others in the personnel field. He also told me that an investigation was going to be conducted examining those of us who had the highest scores. This meant me and most of my people. I knew that we had not taken the test booklet from the locked file cabinets as it was not necessary for us to achieve the high scores that we had attained. This was because I had taken this same test from the first year it was given and my score was within the top five percent army wide. Also study guides are published and are available to anyone interested. On the day we were to be examined, I told each of my people just to tell them the truth and everything would be fine. I was the last to be examined. I was asked to account for why my troops all had very high grades. I answered that I could not understand why I did not have a perfect score and would like to know the one or two questions that I missed. I continued that I had taken the same test from the first year it was given and was awarded proficiency pay from the beginning, and could remember most of the questions on the test with the aid of the study guides and that we met at my house two nights per week and studied. This seemed to satisfy the board and we were all dismissed. I have my own thoughts about the missing test, but since I had no proof of my suspicions I kept my mouth closed on this. I believed that a Sergeant Galewaler who had been transferred overseas just prior to the testing period had taken it with him. As I said, I had no proof of this and this is the first time it is being expressed either orally or in writing.

While my children had Leroy, there were several incidents involving the car. One such incident was that Eva was driving along Sanborn Street while going over the viaduct approaching Abbott Street, there are several traffic lights. It appears that Eva applied the gas pedal instead of the brake and was going too fast to negotiate the turn onto Abbott Street causing most of the lights to be knocked off line and a traffic sign to be sheared off at the base. My children were all taught that if they were in trouble, they were to call home first, because from home they would get the most help. By the time I arrived at the accident, the police were there and the vehicle had been moved out of the line of traffic. My first question was whether or not anyone was hurt and was relieved that only property was damaged, mostly being Leroy. I produced proof of insurance sufficient to cover the damage and everyone went home. Eva said to me when we arrived home, "Thank You Daddy for not being too upset over this accident". I was just relieved that no one was hurt, especially her. About the same time James ran into a telephone pole with his MG which was a total loss. I did not have to go to this accident because James was then old enough to take care of it himself.

During football season one year, Robert had some of his team visiting. As they talked and kidded around, I noticed that one by one they would go outside only to return after very little time had passed. I knew that they were sneaking drinks of alcohol, so I called them all together and told them to go outside and get all of it and place it on the table. They were puzzled as to my motives but they obeyed. There was more than I thought would be. I then told them it was alright to drink however I was going to examine each and every one before leaving the house. If I thought that they had drank too much, that person would remain overnight and I would call his parents and let them know he was here. If I thought he was sober enough to drive, then after drinking a cup of coffee, he could leave. They all agreed and I let the party begin. This occurred during the early nineteen seventies but now that laws have been passed I would not have had the option to allow teenaged drinking at my home. During the party some others who had not been invited tried to crash the party. When I was informed of this by Eva, I started to go and ask them to leave my yard as they had not been allowed into the house. Before I could do this, some of the larger football players said they would take care of it. They calmly went outside and calmly talked to the party crashers who left immediately. I asked them what they told them and was told they said. "If you mess this up for us, you will live to regret it because we will pound you into pulp." A recent law was passed in California making it a crime permitting under-age drinking in one's home.

Robert came to me one day and asked if I would sign for him to use a school musical instrument. He said that he wanted to learn to play the trumpet. This was another opportunity to teach my children about life so I told him that I would sign the slip acknowledging responsibility for the trumpet. I let him know that we always supported things that were worthwhile. There was a premier trumpet player by the name of Harry James who conducted his own band. I told Robert that I did not expect him to be so good at playing his trumpet that Harry James would fear for his job. All his mother and I expected was that a noise that could be called music emanated from his horn. As with all boys, he was horsing around with his friends one day and the trumpet was damaged. It looked as if it had been run over by a car but I was not sure. My children were taught that if there was trouble, come home with it because there is the place more help would come from. Robert brought me the damaged trumpet and told me that it was damaged because he was negligent and did not take care of it, which was the truth. I thought sure that I would have to purchase a new horn for the school but my child told me that it could be fixed at Gadsby's Music Store, so we took the horn there. They acknowledged that they could indeed repair the trumpet and that it was not so costly to repair it. This was music to my ears. They also told us that we could rent a horn while his was being repaired. I was very grateful for this information.

My legacy that I left at Ford Ord was the "Welcome Center". I envisioned a place where a newly arriving soldier could come and have all of his/her in- processing taken care of in one place instead of having to run all over the post, often getting lost. I wrote a paper to the senior staff, endorsed by the Adjutant General, outlining in detail all other agencies that would be involved. Our portion of this venture only entailed personnel assignment to units on the post; yet there were travel and pay to be considered; housing if he/she needed housing for dependents and even sometimes medical. The senior staff thought this was a very good idea and it was almost immediately adopted and the "Welcome Center" was born. One of my senior NCO's, by the name of Lorenzo Muriel had recently gotten into trouble. Although he had a hot temper and angered easily, he was a very good man. He previously was in charge of the Transfer Point, a place where soldiers were separated from the service and/or transferred into the reserves. One little soldier thought that he was out of the army since it was his last day. He would not obey his instructions so Muriel threw him down the steps. In order to determine Muriel's punishment, the headquarters commander asked the advice of the Sergeants Major of Personnel Division and me. We advised the commander to levy a medium sized fine upon him and to relieve him from the job at the Transfer Point. I said that he could be assigned to me and that I had a job for him overseeing the newly organized Welcome Center. Muriel did a fine job and had no further trouble.

Eva had a friend that lived three doors down from our home, whose name was Carol Ramos. They were typical teenaged girls that liked to flirt with boys. One evening Eva and Carol were out on the north side of town flirting with boys when something happened to the car Carol was driving that broke the left headlight. Carol was afraid to go home for fear that her father would go into a rage, so Eva had her bring the car to our house. I had always taught our children to come home when there was any kind of trouble or if they could not, call home and let us know. It so happened that nothing much was wrong with the car that could not be fixed with little or no trouble, so I went and bought a new seal beam and installed it in about thirty minutes.

I am beginning to display anger due to the Agent Orange affect on my brain, although my home life is going beautifully. I am disenchanted also with the army and am leaning toward retirement in that I have served more than twenty years. I am beginning to get uncontrollably angry whenever I feel that I am being slighted or I am confronted with a situation that makes me feel inferior. The Department of Defense wants to close Fort Ord because they believe that it is too costly to run. Again I am called upon to serve on a team whose aim is to save the post from closure. The team is to present a series of briefings. The first briefing will be to the Commanding General of the post for his approval and/or to make minor revisions or additions. The next Briefing is to the Commanding General, Sixth US Army for his approval and then to the Department of the Army. My job on the team is to compile the necessary statistics, many of which cannot be gotten from reports submitted routinely to the command. We worked on the project both day and night, going home exhausted whenever we could take a break. I found myself running around having my people counting first one thing and then another so that I could compile these counting. When the briefing came together we practice it over and over until it was as we thought perfect. The first briefing was made only to find that we had to add some more statistics into it. We breezed through the second briefing and made the final briefing successfully. When all the briefing was over, the Adjutant General called all of his senior NCOs into his office and gave us all a dressing down and reassigned all of us to different jobs. I then found myself without a job. I did not understand this because over the time of the briefings, I was working very hard with him and on several occasions he had told me that I did not have time to look after my branch. Then anger took over and as I was cleaning out my desk I found my retirement application that I had started once before so I completed it and took my final physical examination for retirement. The doctors wanted me to go before a medical review board to determine my disability. My anger was so uncontrollable that I told the doctor to just sign the form that I was alright. Had I not been angry I would have realized that I was waiving some of my rights to compensation for the injuries that I had received from the wars in Korea and Vietnam. I then took my completed retirement application to Sixth US Army at San Francisco. I called upon the personnel there that I had worked with to have my orders issued immediately. I brought my orders back to Fort Ord, gave copies to the appropriate persons and then went home. Years later I would regret this rash action because it became harder for me to obtain just compensation. When I told my darling wife what I had done, as always she stood beside me and said that everything would be alright. Although I had not been separated from the Army, I went to work for GAC Finance in Seaside the next day. I had been working for GAC Finance for about six months when I met, along the street of Marina, the Adjutant General under whom I had worked. He asked me where I had disappeared to and why I retired in such a hurry. I told him that when he moved everyone around that left me without a job, I became angry and retired. He told me that the change was for my benefit to give me space to work with computers and find a way to have any statistic that would be needed, at hand. Well! I said, "You did not tell me". I was retired now, so there was no going back.

Our children are growing up now and our thoughts turn toward college. Nobi and I have never kept our financial condition from our children, so they know and understand that we cannot pay for their college. James, while attending Hartnell Community College, excelled in track and field, especially the long jump and was awarded an athletic scholarship to the University of Arizona. Eva began to attend Hartnell but soon decided not to continue due to her illness. She opted to get a job and experience life because she knew that she was not going to live very much longer. Robert was attending high school and participated in track and light weight football. Robert also played his trumpet in the school band while Judy attended junior high (now called middle school).

One day while visiting Frank Myers, who had also retired from the service, our conversation turned to attendance at church services. He informed me that he had found a small church that was very good that serviced mostly Japanese people. He asked me to attend services with him on the next Sunday. I agreed and Nobi and I went with Frank and his wife Hideko the very next Sunday. We liked it and continued to attend services there regularly. While attending services at Lincoln Avenue Presbyterian Church, we made the acquaintance of Masako Fonner and her husband Bob. We became friends with them and soon found that our children had attended school with their children; and that they lived on the next street over from our house, making us neighbors.

I was getting disenchanted with working at GAC Finance for two reasons: First because I always paid my bills and lived with what money was left, I thought everyone did the same. Second our manager made loans to people who had little or no resources to repay the loan. I did not like chasing after people to make their payments on time. My character would not allow me to quit either so I went about working the best that I could, however, my relationship with the manager became strained as time passed. There was a restaurant nearer the street by our parking lot where "ladies of the night" displayed their wares after our office closed. One time when anger with the manager for his laxity in making loans I said to him, "Why don't you cash a large check and sit at a table near our door and specialize in small loans to customers of the ladies". "We stand the same chance of getting it back". From this time on I was sure that he would get rid of me as soon as he could. Soon after the district office informed us that the company policy had changed so we could not accept partial payments and that all accounts had to be brought up to date. As our business grew smaller, we soon had to reduce our staff by one person. I knew it would be me and I did not care, however the manager did not tell me until my last day. He thought I was going to raise a fuss but I just cleaned out my desk and left. On my way home I stopped in the J.C. Penney store and put in an application for employment and was accepted the next day. I had no opportunity to receive unemployment compensation.

Chapter 13

EMPTYING NEST

Our children seem to be growing up rather fast now. James graduated from Hartnell Community College and received a track scholarship to the University of Arizona at Tucson. Eva graduated from high school, started to go to Hartnell but after one semester decided to work instead because afflicted with Lupus, she realized she would not live very long. She obtained a job working as a sales clerk at The Emporium here in Salinas' Northridge Mall. Robert graduated from high school and enrolled at Hartnell. Although he officially resided at home, he spent a lot of nights with his friends at an apartment on Nacional Street near Hartnell. Eva soon asked to move out and live with some of her girlfriends. Nobi was adamant against her moving fearing that she would spend too much time around boys. She asked for and received a family meeting where she placed her desires before the family and each member voted with Nobi and I having veto power. When Eva was asked why she wanted to move, she said, "I know that I am not going to live very much longer and I just want to see if I am able to live on my own. If I stay home, I will never know whether I can take care of myself". The family gave her unanimous approval and we all helped her pack and move in with her friends. Now the only one of our children that is home is Judy who is beginning high school.

 Nobi received a telephone call from her younger brother that her mother was very sick. She decided that she wanted to go to Japan to see her, as it was during the summer and she was off from work. She found a group that would be travelling to Japan, who would help her with the visas and other travel documents. The weather was hot and muggy in Japan so she had to purchase clothing suitable for wear there. On the day she was to leave, I took her to San Francisco where she joined the group and boarded the airplane. I watched the plane take off and lumber out of site. Right-away I felt lonely but tried not to show it especially after I returned home. In Japan she stayed with her younger brother because there was friction with her older brother. I never found out what this was all about but theorized that it was because she had become Americanized and would not obey him.

A coworker named Bill and I were the only men working in the hardware department of J.C. Penney Company. I had decided that I would at least have fun while working there because they were not paying me enough money to eke out a good living. If I had not been receiving Army retirement pay and Nobi was not working, I could not afford to work there. Now Bill did not like to do anything but work on the register so when he was asked to put together a display he would complain that that was not his job; however when I was asked to do this, I cheerfully said that I would and started right away. If I did not want to do this, I never told the Department Manager, but say that I would cheerfully, go into the stock room, scatter everything from the box around and leave it until the department manager finished the job. Sometimes I would even start assembling the display before I left it. When the department manager was nearly finished, I would come back as if I was going to finish it. The department manager never caught on to my tactics; however if it was Bill, he would make him complete the job.

Once when I had night duty, the Merchandise Manager, a boss higher than the Department Manager, asked me to try to sell some Aluminum Yard Sheds that had been opened and spread around. My instructions were to get as much as I could, and if I could not sell them by a certain date, I was to put everything into the trash pactor. After examining the buildings, I saw an opportunity to get a building for myself, my next door neighbor and even some of the employees. He did not tell me how much of a discount to give. The buildings were an eyesore and some important people from the main office were coming to visit the store, so to get rid of what he deemed trash was my main object. I immediately called my next door neighbor who owned a truck and told him to come to the store because I had aluminum buildings for sale very cheap. I also told him he had to take mine home for me. Before the night was over I had disposed of all the buildings and had building maintenance come and clean up the area. The Merchandise Manager was very happy that the job was completed so soon.

Alisal High School where Judy was a student had a marching band. Judy joined the band, playing the clarinet. The band was very good and won several awards. Nobi and I went to their events just as when the boys were playing football or running track. There were times when we went out of town with the band. I became president of the band boosters when Judy was a senior and remained on the job for a year after she graduated. Eva had been dating a boy by the name of Edward Dubrovnic, a military police at Fort Ord. It was about this time that he asked her to marry him and she said, "yes". We had no objections to him as he was a very nice boy of half Japanese extraction; however his mother had some objections to Eva but never said exactly what she objected to. Edward did not let her objections deter him as he really wanted to marry Eva. One thing Eva did not know was that Nobi and I would have paid for her wedding. Our children were so used to doing for themselves that Eva was saving money from each of her pay checks from working at The Emporium.

I was asked if I could rewire the grid displaying the electrical fixtures on sale at the J.C. Penney store where I worked. As I set up my work bench to begin changing the light fixtures, Bill came to me and said that I was crazy to do this for the store. He said that if I did not do it, they would have to hire an electrician. I told him I did not care about such things, that I would enjoy doing this more than working on the register. As I removed the old fixture I found that some had been accidently damaged during the course of doing business. I found that some of the broken lamps could be put together and made great looking lamps. I did make a few lamps from the broken ones but since they did not have a stock number they could not be sold and I was told that I could have any that I made. One is still hanging in our family room. It took several weeks to complete the job so I was happy that no one would bother me while I worked on the grid.

As time passed Eva was spending more and more time as a patient in the hospital. After a hospital stay she called home and asked if she could come back home. We told her that she could always come home so I went to their apartment and brought her home. Her pain from the lupus was growing worse and the doctors could not do very much for her, in fact they informed us that anything could happen anytime now. The doctor put her back in the hospital because there they could give her stronger medicine that she could take at home. I give her doctors credit for preparing her for her soon demise because she took the news very calmly. One day she wanted to come home but the nurses would not let her. Then Eva began to cry so they told her she had to be back at the hospital by five o'clock PM. Eva came home and said good bye to her dog and took her last look at everything she wanted to see and at five o'clock she returned to the hospital. At nine thirty PM August 31, 1975 our Eva departed this earth. Nobi and I were very distraught with grief. James was still away at college. I had to call and inform him of his sister's death and told him to come home. Our other children were either at home or close by so we were all here at home. It was very difficult to make her final arrangements so we asked Syl and Lorraine from next door to help us. They went with me when I purchased her grave site at Queen of Heaven Cemetery which is situated on a hill. I found the perfect place. The grave site was in a perfect line with our house. After the funeral and burial, Nobi was home still crying when she said that she was sure that Edwards mother was happy that Eva had died so that Edward would not marry her. This only made matters worse for her and was very hard to calm her. I had my own situation. I had been lying down but was not sleep. I heard the telephone ringing and went to answer it. Of course I was the only one to hear it ring. When I picked up the receiver, a voice said to me, "This is Salinas Valley Memorial Hospital, come up and get your daughter because she is doing cartwheels up and down the halls and is disturbing the other patients. I started out the door enroute to the hospital. Our sons asked where I was going and when I said I was going to the hospital to get Eva, it took both sons to prevent me from leaving the house. I soon realized that it was to let me know that Eva was alright wherever she was. Being a Christian, my belief is that she is in Heaven.

    I worked for J.C. Penney store for a few more months, then an old friend and mentor came to the store and told me that he had a job for me. I knew he was the Data Processing Manager at Granite Construction Company. He told me that I had an appointment with Brian Kelley, the manager of Pipeline and Plant Division of the company on Monday morning. I was interviewed and accepted for the job, which paid much more than I was earning at the Penney store. I soon learned that I was right back into high stressed jobs. Seems as though I attract jobs that take a heavy toll on my body and mind. Since the branch was beginning to bid jobs by computer I had to train the estimators. They were fast learners so it was not long before we were ready for our first bid using the computer. After I had worked there about a year I learned that we could add the labor burden to the labor rate file which would greatly improve the accuracy of the bid. We made other changes to the system that dealt with trenching and backfilling.

Times seem to pass rapidly now. Nobi was still working at Sherwood School in the cafeteria, James had graduated from the university and was teaching high school in Tucson; Robert was attending Cal Poly in San Luis Obispo and Judy was at Hartnell working on their police force. Judy was interested in being in law enforcement. It would not be long before all our children left the nest. Robert was going with a girl named Barbara Reed at the time. She went with Robert to San Luis Obispo, and lived in a small house on Perkins Lane. Our finances are now much better and we are able to save much of our income. Our children are doing a good job of working and paying for their own college cost without going into debt. Nobi and I started a new family tradition. At Christmas time we put together a box containing things that our children could not afford to buy and gave it as a present. This tradition continues until now even though our children can afford anything they want, because they enjoyed the gesture.

I had been working at Granite Construction for about a year when the stress of the job began to take its toll on my body. It was during this time that I suffered the second of my Transient Ischemic Attacks (TIA), which are miniature strokes. I suffered the first one during my military service at Fort Ord. I was printing the first run of a bid which always contained errors. To easily identify errors, the program will remove any calculations made and fill the number field with a series of ones. As the bid was printing I was standing over the printer looking for places that contained the series of ones so that I could mark them with a magic marker and correct them. When I suffered the TIA I lost conscience and had fallen over the printer where I was found. I was rushed to the hospital but did not stay long because the TIA eases after about an hour or so. I was sent home to rest for the remainder of the day, or until I felt better. This caused some concern to my supervisors because the bid had to be completed by a specific hour and date.

Nobi and I started to take short trips since we could now afford to do so and because our children were leaving home to be on their own. We started with two or three day trips to places like Reno and Las Vegas with tour companies. These trips did not cost much because almost everything was included in the initial price. We found these trips fun and soon joined other groups that specialized in tour travel. After teaching for two years at the high school in Tucson, James quit because he said that they would not let him teach like he wanted. He moved to Sacramento and bought a taco business called "Mr. Taco". Judy graduated from Hartnell and soon followed James to Sacramento, working at his business. Being siblings, this did not last long and Judy moved out of his house and rented her own place. She stayed in Sacramento attending Sacramento State University studying Criminal Justice. She also got a job on the university police force there, mostly because she had previous experience.

Nobi and I are mostly alone at home now so we started travelling sometimes with groups, other times alone. Sometimes we drove our car or went by airplane. We began taking our annual trip to Little Rock to visit my parents. On our first trip to Hawaii, we purchased a timeshare condo with two bedrooms, complete with kitchen and baths. With this purchase we joined a club that would allow us to share other facilities. Since we both still worked, we could only do most of our travelling during the summer when school was not in session and I could take vacation time. We also travelled to visit our children on weekends as they were about three hours' drive away. Due to the stress at work, together with the injury to my brain and lungs from the Agent Orange I suffered in Vietnam my anger increased to the point that I needed help but did not recognize it at the time. While driving from visiting our children one day on a crowded highway, I followed the car ahead from a safe distance. If another car violated my space, I got so angry that I would get as close to that car as possible in order to force him out of my lane. Nobi, being non-confrontational would scream at me but I would not hear her. Every time we went to visit our children this would happen until one day after arriving at our freeway exit at John Street, I said, "We are home now". She answered with a small voice barely audible, "Yes, but I was scared every step of the way. In fact, every time I have to go somewhere with you, I believe it will be my last day on this earth". This I heard. I really felt bad at what my wife thought. From that time on, I could hear her saying that to me and I knew I had to do something about it. At first, like always, I tried to do it myself and I did make a little progress. Every time I had to go out, I practiced being patient with all other drivers even if they were in the wrong. Nobi soon took notice that I was trying to change and tried to help me. I get professional help after an incident at work. We had made additions to our office building making it twice as large. My computer room was given larger space in the new addition. One night, while working very late, I was trying to get the first run on a bid ready for review the next morning. I missed an error and had to run the whole bid over which would take about another hour. I got so mad that I kicked the new wall but soon calmed myself and did what I could to repair it. The next day another person was blamed for damaging the wall and was going to be fired. I could not let this happen, so I went to the manager and told him that I was the one who damaged the wall and why I did it. He happened to know of a great psychologist who could help me and asked me if I wanted him to see if he could get an appointment for me. I spent the next four years getting anger management help.

Chapter 14

OUR TRAVELS (ATLANTIC CITY AND WASHINGTON DC)

Casinos were opening at Atlantic City, New Jersey. Nobi and I planned a trip to Atlantic City and Washington DC. We obtained brochures for each of our destinations together with maps and travel guides from

AAA. The travel documents indicated that in the casinos, men must wear jackets and women dresses. We packed these clothing along with casual attire and the day of our departure, we left for the airport. Our trip to New York was without incident but when we went to the gate for our trip to Atlantic City there was no plane even though the time for the flight was near. The few of us at the gate were a little apprehensive about when and what type of plane would come. After a while a small twin engine aircraft came and we loaded on it. It was so small that there was no place for our carry—on luggage. Either we had room for our feet or our luggage, but not both. When we arrived at Atlantic City, the pilots put our baggage on a rack and locked up the airport. There were no cabs there and when one did come, it was to pick up a specific passenger who had ordered it before arriving. When the last passenger, other than Nobi and I, got their cab, I asked them if other cabs would be coming. This is when we learned that one had to order a cab. These passengers felt sorry for us since we did not know about the cab situation and they offered to share their cab. We were so grateful that we paid for both our fare and the other passengers. We arrived at Trump Plaza, our hotel, and by the time we were settled in our room we were too late to enter the dining room as it closed at ten o'clock. I knew that Nobi was hungry and had to eat because of her diabetes, so I went looking for something. The only place that I found was a hot dog stand behind the casino near the alley way. I purchased what I could and took it to our room. Now we were ready to go down to the casino and try our luck. Looking around to see what the men and women were wearing, I found that I was the only one wearing a jacket and tie. We did not remain in the casino long because it was apparent that none of the machines were paying and they were costly. Being optimistic, Nobi and I took these setbacks in stride and thought things would be better in the morning when we could explore the area and find things more to our liking.

When we went back to our room we found that our window looked out onto a dirty piece of plastic hanging from the building next door that was under construction. Still we thought things would be better the next morning, so we went to bed and got a good night's sleep. The next morning after we showered, shaved and dressed, this time in casual clothes, we went down for breakfast. Only the coffee shop was open and seemed that everyone in the hotel was trying to crowd into this small place. There were long lines everywhere. Nobi told me that her blood sugar was low since we did not have much to eat the night before, but there was not too much I could do but keep our place in line and wait until we could get a table. It's a good thing that I carry with me sugar pills so I gave her a couple to hold her over until we could eat. When we finally did get a table, we were in a crowded space and we had a hostile waitress. I ordered a simple breakfast of eggs over easy, bacon, toast and tea. Nobi had oatmeal and coffee. I asked our waitress if they could not make perfect toast, under cook mine rather than burn it. When our breakfast came, I looked at my toast and it was golden brown on the top side. I thought things were looking up, but when I turned my toast over, it was burned to a crisp on the underside. Every time I tried to get a waitress's attention, she would tell me that it was not her table, so I just ate my eggs and bacon and we left. The bill was also over—priced, so I did not leave any tip and felt justified. We went out on the boardwalk and found conditions there not much better. Seems as if everyone there was hostile and some kind of battle was being waged with others over jobs. We were told that there had been a group of people who ran rolling chairs to taxi the tourist between casinos along the boardwalk. Some others came with jeeps and trams came and under-cut the price charged because they could carry more passengers; running them out of business. This was none of our concern so we just availed ourselves of what transportation was there. We went into the next casino going south on the boardwalk. There, security confiscated my camera equipment and held it until we were ready to leave. We did not remain long in any of the casinos because it just was not like Las Vegas or Reno. When we were hungry, about noon, we could not find anywhere to eat except an ice cream stand so that is what we had for lunch.

We survived until it was time for the evening meal. We went into the dining room and got the shock of our trip after looking at the menu. The prices started at fifty dollars. We had no other choice because we needed a decent meal. With our meal, drinks and a cheap dessert, our tab came to one hundred and forty seven dollars plus I had to leave an appropriate tip. We had two more days to stay in Atlantic

City so we had to find something else that would entertain us until it was time to leave. Day two of our stay at Atlantic City was almost a carbon copy of day one, except that we only had one more day to spend there. As we were passing through the lobby of the hotel, I saw a booth with a sign over it saying "VIP Information". Since we were guests at the hotel, paying a very high price that made us VIP's. I asked the girl there if she had a booklet advertising what was going on around the town. I almost had to fight her to get one. When she finally relented, I told her that I would go to our room and look it over and bring it back; in that I was sure she had a limited supply. She told me that she had plenty of them. We learned from the booklet that the town of Smithville was nearby and that all we had to do was walk a couple of blocks to the bus station and take a bus there. Luck was with us because the bus was just about to leave when we got there. We spent a lovely day there. Even the cost of food was reasonable. We thought about buying a Smithville ham but decided not to because it would cost too much to ship it to Salinas.

Early the next morning we went to the airport and took the same small plane to Washington DC. After settling in our hotel we walked a few blocks to the railroad/subway station and took a tram to the Capital Mall. We looked at everything on the mall but spent most of the time at the Aeronautical building of the Smithsonian. They had on display airplanes of every era. Being familiar with our airplanes, I spent a lot of time examining the German Messerschmitt ME109 and the Japanese Zeke (Called Zero). We had our lunch in this building and continued looking at everything until late in the evening. Nobi seemed not to be bored but I am sure that spending most of the day in this building was more for my benefit because I am so fond of aircraft and rockets. Of course I have always known that I have a sweet wife. Because it was so late we missed the last tram back to the railroad station. We had no other choice but to try the subway which was easy to understand so we made out alright. We had three more days to spend around Washington DC so we look at everything that we could. We even ate at a Japanese restaurant. On our last day we went to the Vietnam Monument to look for the name of the husband of our next door neighbor Mrs. Devoe. His name was David. After looking for about thirty minutes we found it and made a tracing of it for her. We also took lots of pictures of the mall as well as the Vietnam Monument.

When it was time for us to leave Washington DC we had to board a bus that would take us to Dulles International Airport which was quite a ways out of town. Nobi and I were the only ones on the bus so the driver had time to talk to us while driving the bus. She told us that she was from Atlantic City and that she took a pay cut to leave there. She told us why there was so much hostile feelings among the workers there. Everyone expected more from the casinos. They thought that the casinos were going to pay for the revitalization of the town; but they only remodeled the boardwalk which ran in front of every casino.

Dulles was a strange airport. All of the airplanes were placed out on the tarmac about a half mile from the terminal building. When our flight was called, we boarded trams that took us to the planes. The tram was much lower than the plane so when the tram arrived at the plane, hydraulic jacks lifted the body of the tram even with the entrance to the plane. We then boarded the aircraft and flew to San Francisco and then to home.

Chapter 15

A SAD TIME FOR OUR DAUGHTER

The saddest day in the life of our daughter Judy was one in which she had to bury her husband and while preparing for his funeral, had to put her dog "Shasha" to sleep. Before I get into the sad part, I will regress to a more happy time. Our daughter Judy was a police officer with the city of Hercules in the East Bay of San Francisco, near the City of Richmond California. She met another police officer with the city of Walnut Creek, named William Penquite. The fell in live; became engaged and on August 31, 1996 they were married. It was a happy time and they made plans for the future. Time passed; Bill was promoted to Sergeant; they made plans to move to Colorado, away from the fast life of the San Francisco Bay area. Judy asked for and received a piece of unimproved property Nobi and I owned in Colorado City, a small town south of Pueblo. She also bought the lot adjoining the one we gave to her creating a lot approximately ¾ of an acre. They planned to build a very large two story house on the property and live there after retirement.

Over the years they made several trips to view the property and to check upon the progress of the infrastructure and additions to the city. They also talked to others about the availability of jobs, if they wanted to work after retirement. I have to admit that Nobi and I did not want them to move to Colorado because of the weather there and we did not want to have to travel there for visit. We did not often voice our objections because they were aggressively pursuing their plans. They were buying and storing things for their new home.

Then one morning when we were having our breakfast, we received a phone call from Judy crying that Bill was dead. I asked her what had happened and she said that she was not really sure but she needed us to come. We dropped everything and packed a few things and drove to her home. When we arrived, more information was available. This is how things unfolded. When Bill did not arrive at work, the Walnut Creek Police called Judy inquiring why he did not come to work. Judy went home to find Bill dead while still sitting at the breakfast table preparing for work. There was no indication that he had been murdered or foul play was involved. Their dog Shasha was being treated for cancer at the University of California at Davis. The treatment was not going well at the time. As we were preparing for Bill's funeral; we awoke in the morning to find that Shasha was also dying. Judy had to stop preparing for Bill's funeral to take Shasha to the Veterinarian Department of UC, Davis to be put to sleep. Nobi and I accompanied her on this journey as we were sure that Judy was in much pain and we did not want her travelling alone. After the veterinarian had completed his work and Shasha was sleeping, the pain was too much for Judy who cried her eyes out. When this ordeal was over she still had to return and complete the arrangements for Bill's funeral.

Bill was the kind of man who had many friends, including friends in every police department in the area. Bill also was one who liked to wear "goofy" ties. On the day of his funeral, the men of his extended family all wore the goofy ties in his honor. The large church was overflowing with people. Every police force in the area was represented. During the service several police officers came to the podium and gave tributes to Bill. When the service was over, the motorcade enroute to the cemetery had to pass the freeway interchange at Interstate 80 and Interstate 580. The Highway Patrol stopped traffic on each on ramp until the motorcade had passed. To my knowledge this is never done even for dignitaries. When the short service at the grave site was over and they were lowering the casket into the grave, my two sons had to restrain Judy because she was in so much pain. I hope that I never again see any of my children in this much pain.

This was a very sad time for my daughter. She grieved a long time for both her husband and her dog. Over time things got better and she was able to cope with her life. She continued with her police work until she was injured on the job chasing a person that had broken the law. Her injury to her arm was such that she could not be effective on the job and was retired with a pension.

Chapter 16

OUR GOLDEN WEDDING ANNIVERSARY

As our fiftieth wedding anniversary approached, my love and I started to plan what we were going to do for our anniversary. We could have saved our energy because our children had already taken this task from us and began their own plan. My daughter Judy is very good in planning; making lists, sending out invitations etc. My oldest son James is good in finding elegant places for holding parties. Each of my children had applied their talents and put together our party. They invited family members from around the country, our church members and our friends. My mother, who was in her nineties, could not attend due to ill health. Our children booked the upper floor of Tarpy's Road Side Restaurant for our party. Because I had to do something for our affair, I booked a block of rooms for the "out of town" guest, mostly family members at the "Goodnight Inn" a few blocks from our home, and guaranteed payment with my credit card.

    I wanted to recite our wedding vows during the party but my dear wife said that she knew that I loved her dearly and had been faithful all these years and saw no reason to do this. She said that we should just have a good time for our celebration and not make it look like a wedding; after all we had been married for fifty years. As usual I bowed to her thinking and let go of my idea.

    On the night of the party, we had an open bar during the get acquainted phase for those who did not know each other. Our sit down dinner had several menu selections so that everyone could have what they wanted to eat. Our very good friends, Lisa and Doug McFarland have two daughters that we treated as our own. They had been raised part of their lives in Hawaii and did the hula very well. They danced the hula for us as well as our guests and upon completion, placed the leis around our necks where they remained throughout the remainder of the party. After the show, Doug came and asked me how I had gotten the girls to dance for me. It was the girl's idea but I could not miss a chance to brag, so I told him that I had just asked them. He said that when he asked, it was very difficult for him.

Our son Robert is a member of a small group that makes very good wine, especially wine that is not commercially made by wine masters. Robert wanted to use his wine at the party; however the uncorking fee charged by the restaurant was as much as if we bought it from them, so we bought Champaign and served it along with the cake at the end of the meal. Nobi and I really enjoyed our celebration.

Chapter 17

CRUISE TO THE BAHAMAS

This cruise taught my love and I to pay a nominal price for the things that we get. We answered an advertisement for a very cheap cruise to the Bahamas from the State of Florida with airfare and hotel for two days prior and one day after the cruise all included in the price of $300.00 each. We knew that we would have to listen to a sales pitch for some type of timeshare but since we already owned one they would accept that fact and forgo the sales pitch to us. We were wrong. Upon arriving in Fort Lauderdale we went directly to the car rental place that was designated by the organization and were pressured to purchase a lot of insurance on the rental car. After leaving the car rental establishment we went to our hotel that we had selected from a list they provided. This turned out to be satisfactory although we would not have selected this particular one if we were paying for it. We spent the two allotted days touring around the Miami-Fort Lauderdale area. Although we were not having the best of times, it was satisfactory and sometimes even enjoyable. There were concerts on the beach in the evening after the hot weather cooled down some. On the morning that we were to appear for the sales pitch things went downhill from there. First we were separated from our car by being taken to a park some distance from their office under the guise of not being disturbed. Then a high pressure sales pitch began without letup even though we constantly told them that we already owned one and that if we wanted to come to Florida the exchange program under the timeshare program that we already owned would allow us to come to the one they were selling. This went on for hours but in the end we still did not purchase another timeshare.

The next afternoon we went to the ship for the cruise because the timeshare people had promised this in writing so they could not back out. Everyone around us on the cruise was angry over the way they were treated during the sales pitch. We understood from speaking to others that very few timeshares were sold. The boat was nice and very large. Although we only had an inside cabin, we did not expect one on the upper decks. There was the usual amount of food that just looking at it made you gain weight. We were served three full meals daily plus the midnight snack that amounted to the fourth meal because everything was on the buffet. I took many, many pictures of the boat inside and out as well as in Nassau; but could not find them even after searching through every nook and cranny of our house.

I was kind of impressed with the way they built their houses. Their houses were completely concrete, even the roof and painted pastel colors of pink and blue mostly. Sometimes someone would paint their houses yellow while others would leave it white. As I understand it, they have made their houses hurricane resistant. When hurricanes comes through their island very little is destroyed. Looking at New Orleans after Hurricane Katrina I fail to see why the people there and other gold coast cities do not adopt the idea of building homes of concrete.

As Nobi and I walked around in Nassau we met a fellow selling tee shirts. We did not want to buy any of his or any other tee shirts; but we did engage him in conversation. As we talked, the subject came around to welfare and the people who received it. He seemed proud that everyone there worked, even old people, if they wanted to eat. He also stated that in our country we give too much money and goods free to people on welfare. We also did not want to buy anything expensive because we were not sure of the taxing upon our return to the states. We had heard that some goods marked as "duty free" in fact did have a tax and besides anything we were interested in, we could get at home.

Chapter 18

TRAVEL WITH MY PARENTS

Its summer again; Nobi is off from work; I am on vacation from work so we decided to invite my parents to accompany us on our second trip to Hawaii since they had never been there. I had never travelled with my parents and did not know how it would workout. My mother and father would have to travel from Little Rock to California and would be tired by the time they arrived at our house. We scheduled some time for them to rest before embarking on another long journey. When it was time to leave, we drove to San Francisco and parked in one of the long term parking lots where the car would be protected and they would bus us to the air terminal. We boarded the plane and flew to Honolulu arriving in the mid afternoon. The only difference between this trip and our first trip was that Nobi and I were alone; we had purchased a time share condominium that was equipped with two bedrooms, a full kitchen and two baths. We were using the condo for the first time since acquiring it. We knew that it was a short distant from the city but since we did not know exactly where it was; we also had to rent a car and it was late in the afternoon by the time we were settled, so we stayed in the first night and rested.

The next morning after we had breakfast, as we were leaving, the people occupying the condo next to ours were also leaving. After "good morning" pleasantries were over we agreed to meet them in town at a bar that was situated under a very large oak tree. We found the place and our new friends were already there so we joined them. We were all drinking some kind of blue Hawaiian drink that had very little alcohol, except Mama who had a soft drink. Even Nobi was drinking them without effect. We would take turns buying rounds of drink for the whole table. We could have been there drinking all day without even feeling the effects of the drinks, but after two or three rounds, Mama started telling each of us how many drinks we had had. I was so embarrassed that I had to get up from the table and go inside. It was not long before we left the bar and went sightseeing.

During our stay there, we shopped around Waikiki beach buying trinkets to bring home. As we were shopping around we saw a pretty little girl who was half Hawaiian and half Japanese. We were so taken by her beauty and her friendliness that we told her that we were going to take her back home with us. Of course we were just kidding her. We also went to Waimea Park where Mom and Dad were awed by the beautiful flowers, bushes, waterfalls and ponds. We spent the whole day there. At night we went to a luau. After eating some of the roast pig and all of the other goodies that they had prepared for us, they put on a show. After the hula dancers had done their numbers, the girls came into the audience and picked out a man each to come onto the stage and hula. Of course I got picked and went on the stage and made a fool of myself, but all in fun. It's a good thing there were no pictures because I was the one that took all of the pictures. The next day we went to the Kodak Hula Show and spent the whole day looking at the hula dancers perform. They looked very good in their different costumes and dances.

The next day we went to the Polynesian Culture Center and spent the whole day there. From our condo it was quite a long drive to the south west corner of the island. Each of the Polynesian islands was represented with a display of what life is like on their island. We found that very interesting seeing the different peoples and how they lived. There were also shows for us to see and plenty of things to buy. Most of the costumes and the beautiful girls were something to see as they floated down the canal. The men were impressive also. This parade went on almost all of the day. At night there were parties and food everywhere. Of course we had to pay to eat and drink. We were having such a good that we stayed well after dark and had a difficult time trying to drive back to the condo but it was well worth it. Nobi and I had been to see the culture center on our first visit but it was still great to see it again. Mom and Dad really enjoyed everything.

Our next adventure was to the Arizona Memorial where the Battleship Arizona was sunk at Pearl Harbor at the beginning of World War II. There were long lines waiting to board the shuttle craft that ferried us to the sunken battleship. Once there we looked around at the various displays; took some pictures and read some of the names of the sailors that went down with the ship. We did not stay there long because Mom and Dad said that it was kind of a sad event to see what happened to the sailors that went down with the ship. When we arrived back on shore, we went into town and spent the rest of the day shopping.

We next ventured to Waimea Park. My parents were used to flowers as they have many of their own at their home in Little Rock; however they were carried away when they saw the flowers in the park.

They were thrilled at the size of the exotic plants, most of which they had never seen. Of course many of the plants are native to the Hawaiian Islands and the surrounding area. We spent the whole day there just looking at the plants and water falls. I had never seen my parents so excited over flowers and bushes. I can still hear my mother calling to my father, "James, come and look at this". Other places we had gone they would only say, "That's nice" or, "That's kind of pretty". It was just like my mother to start talking to perfect strangers about the plants and bushes saying how she wished she could get plants like these to grow in her yard back home. I told her that she could not even get the fuchsia in my yard to grow. Nobi and I took cuttings from our fuchsia rooted and potted it and took it to her on three separate occasions, and each time it died as soon as winter came. No way was she going to get these tropical plants to grow anywhere it gets cold.

Our seven days went by very fast and before we knew it, it was time for us to leave and come home. We drove back to the Honolulu Airport, turned in the car and boarded our flight back to San Francisco. From there we drove home to Salinas and rest for Mom and Dad. After resting for a couple of days, my love and I took Mom and Dad to Judy's house. At that time she had rented a house in Vallejo and was working as a campus police officer for the university where she attended school. From there we took them to Sacramento where James had a fast food business called "Mr. Taco". We sat around and watched James work while eating his tacos. We drove Mom and Dad back to Salinas. The next day we drove down to San Luis Obispo to see Robert and Barb. They took Mom and Dad on a tour of the area so that my parents could see how they lived. It was soon time for my parents to fly back to Little Rock.

When I returned to work after my vacation, things began to change for me. Large construction projects had slowed considerably. The few that were put out for bid now had more bidders so jobs were harder to win. My health also had deteriorated in that the strain of fierce bidding caused me to suffer my third TIA (Transient Ischemic Attack) and the branch manager was beginning to fear that I would die on the job although I continually went to see my therapist. Another thing that caused me distress was that we had won a bid and had a little party. One of the Vice Presidents came over to our branch and drank too much. I was the last to understand what was happening and found that everyone had slipped away and I was left with him. He did not remain on the company property but went down town to bars leaving unpaid bills that I went behind him and paid for his continued drinking. The next morning when I went to work I was called into the branch manager's office and was asked what happened the night before. I do not know how anyone found out because I was the only one who knew and I did not tell anyone. I told the branch manager that so far as I was concerned nothing had happened. He would not let it go so literally I was brow beaten until I gave in and told what had happened. From this time I was not comfortable going to the main office because the Vice President could not look me in the face. I was beginning to realize that if our branch was consolidated with Heavy Engineering Branch, I would not be retained so I began to bring home samples of the systems that I had programmed. During the year I noticed that some of our key people were leaving the company. From that I concluded that the consolidation was going to take place and that I would most likely be out of a job.

The next summer when I took vacation, we asked my parents to go to Acapulco. Again Mom and Dad came to San Francisco where Nobi and I met them for the drive to Salinas. When I saw my dad, I was surprised that he had become very frail and did not have the energy that he had the year before. I had made all of the arrangements for our trip. We drove back to San Francisco; parked at the same parking lot and took the shuttle to our airline. Upon arrival in Acapulco we went directly to our hotel. When we checked in, they made a mistake and gave me a key that would open every door on our floor. I did not know this until I too made a mistake. We settled mom and dad in their room but thought Nobi's and mine would be next door so I opened that door only to find people in the room. Our room was across the hall. We did not rent a car this time because the hotel provided transportation to most places their guest wanted to go. Being in Mexico, we were being extra careful not to eat or drink anything that was not made at the hotel.

Our hotel was right on the beach so we could see many sights from the balcony of our rooms. There was always something going on in the water below. This was our first time to see parasailing where people on water skis with a parachute strapped on them are being pulled by a motor boat. The faster the boat went, the higher the skier rose above the water. There were also people on jet skis along with an assortment of boats. Of course there were people lounging around on the beach doing nothing. These things were good to look at, but our thing was to go into the city and look around.

   One such place we went to was Cathedral Square where we took lots of pictures of this church. There was always shopping no matter where we went. When I look back at some of the pictures of our trips, I am delighted to see how happy the love of my life was and how she enjoyed going on these trips. I am sure that this fact was one of the reasons that I took such care in planning these trips. One day we went to see the Quebrada Cliff Divers. I bet it took guts to dive off of these high cliffs because they had to time their dives so that the waves were coming in and the water was deep enough. We were told that if the water was not right, the divers could be severely injured or possibly killed. Also the divers had to make their dive so that they would clear the mountain itself; which means that the divers had to dive out from the mountain. When we were kids, we used to go swimming in bauxite mines that had filled with water. These mines were very deep so we would climb up into the nearby trees and dive into the water; I would never try anything like the feats of the cliff divers. Of course now I have more sense.

One day we went on a tour that took us to another beach where the water was much warmer and the waves were much gentler. It was such a nice place that my mother, dressed in a knee length dress, complete with stockings went wading into this water. She did take off her high heeled shoes and stockings. Before the day was over she was wet up to her waist. We were having a lot of fun except my dad who just sat in the shade under a tree. This was when Nobi and I really noticed how frail and listless he was. We asked him if something was wrong but all he would say was that he was just kind of tired. Because we were on a tour bus, we could not leave so that he could go to the hotel and lie down. I also want to mention that my dear wife got the bottom of her shorts wet too. I was smart enough not to go too far out into the water and only got my feet wet. When we did get back to the hotel we were all tired and went to our rooms for a nap before we went out for our night life at the Culture Center where there were many Mexican dances as well as Indian dances with elaborate costumes of many varieties.

One day after we had been shopping, it was so hot this particular day that we began sweating immediately upon leaving the shuttle bus, I went into the hotel bar and ordered four pina collata drinks. Honest to goodness I had no devilment motive in my action, but was driven by the weather when I ordered the drinks. I just did not think about my mother not drinking alcohol. I brought the drinks over to the table where my family had sat and passed out the drinks. Likewise my mother was also driven by the weather because she drank hers down in two or three swallows like it was water. Then she looked at me and said, "You did something to my drink". It was then I realized that I had given my mother alcohol. No matter what I said, she believed that I did that on purpose.

We spent another day at Marine World of Acapulco. It had all of the shows and exhibits that are contained at Marine World in San Diego. We still enjoyed going there watching the dolphins perform as well as the killer whales. We were careful not to get too close and get wet; we left this to the young.

We had been so careful not to eat or drink anything outside of the hotel, unless it had been sold in bottles or had been heated high enough to kill any bacteria. On our last day we went into the hotel dining room and had ice cream as it was hot and we wanted to cool off a bit. Sure enough we all got sick enough to vomit everything from our stomachs. We then remembered that the ice cream was not made at the hotel and that the milk used might have been contaminated. The next day we came home landing in San Francisco and driving down to Salinas. I still had a few days of vacation so we took Mom and Dad to visit out children. We went first to visit Judy who lived in Vallejo and worked as a police officer. Judy does not like to have pictures taken of her but made one with her grandmother. The next day we went to visit Robert and Barb so that mom could see how they lived. Since Mom and Dad were due to leave the next day, we stayed overnight and drove them to the Los Angeles International Airport where they took a flight home.

My vacation time was over and when I went to work on Monday morning, things had changed considerably. The merger of our branch into Heavy Engineering was to take place and I was told not to start any projects so I knew that I had lost my job. I also knew that the decision to not retain me in some other capacity in the company since I had been an exceptional employee was due to my making the Vice President very uncomfortable. I was told by others in the company that there had been discussions over whether I would put up a fuss or threaten suit but I had no such ideas but went quietly. I tried to start my own business but when I advertised my availability to do computer contract bidding, I was sued by the company citing proprietary information. My therapist knew a good lawyer who wrote a letter shaming them into dropping the charges. I then got a job in San Mateo, a city near San Francisco, with Responsive Data Systems. Not only did I receive more pay, but I learned to be a much better programmer working with so many different projects.

When I interviewed for the job at Responsive Data Systems, I took the job on condition that I could find an apartment in the area. During the weekend before I was to start to work, Nobi and I went apartment hunting. On the second try we found a two bedroom place. Soon after beginning work, I met Joan Armani and Larry Fullerton and we became friends as well as coworkers. I had been there for about two months when Larry made a bad mistake with a woman. He bought a motor home together with this woman and her grown son, mostly with Larry's money, but the motor home somehow was put into the woman's name. At their first disagreement, they threw Larry out so he had nowhere to go. I told him that I had an extra bedroom and that if he could stand me, he could come and live with me. This would also help with the rent. We got along very well and could share rides to work. I did most of the cooking while Larry did the shopping. We decided to take up square dancing where Larry met the love of his life. I still cannot believe that I went square dancing.

After I had been working there for a while, I started to drive up to San Mateo on Sunday evening because I had made a deal with the boss that I would come in very early each morning to start the computer so that the programmers could start work immediately. This way I could leave to come to Salinas after work on Thursday. Nobi knew that Joan and I were just friends so there was no problem for me to spend time with her. Joan had visited us at our home in Salinas and had spent time with us when Nobi came to stay with me during the summer months when she was not working. One Sunday afternoon after driving to San Mateo I decided to stop by Joan's apartment. We began drinking and watching television. I did not want to go to my apartment because I would be alone. Larry and the love of his life had gotten their own place. I did not notice that Joan was beginning to get a little drunk and lonely at the same time until she made a pass at me. The first time she did this I let it pass but when she made another pass, I told her that it was time for me to go to my place and left. The next morning she told me that she was very glad that I had the strength not to take advantage of the situation of the last evening. From that time, every time she had a date, she asked Larry and me to pass judgment on the guy to see if he was sincere. Eventually the right guy did come along. Nobi and I even double dated with them.

The next year Nobi and I decided to take Mom and dad on a trip to Las Vegas, since we could use our timeshare there without additional cost. In addition we made reservations to fly to the Grand Canyon for a day or two and return to Las Vegas. Before I could get all of the arrangements made, I received a call from my mother that my father was dying of cancer and that I should come to Little Rock immediately. Nobi was not feeling well either and I did not want to leave her home alone so she said that she would go to Little Rock with me. We went to the San Francisco airport to get a flight. The attendant that checked us in felt so sorry for us that the airline could not help us with the cost because our bereavement was not verified by the Red Cross, so she put us in first class without the additional cost. When we arrived at Little Rock, it was during the winter months and it was cold. As soon as I stepped off the plane, it felt as if I did not have on my pants. I had to look down to make sure I was clad appropriately. When Nobi and I arrived at my Mom's home, we learned that my father had passed. After comforting my mother I put Nobi to bed because she was feeling worse. During our stay I helped my mother with the funeral arrangement while my nieces worked on the obituary. It was a nice service and the Masonic Temple put on a display after the funeral as my father had held a high position.

When Nobi and I returned home I continued to make arrangements for our trip to Las Vegas. My sister Melba would accompany mom on the trip. Mom and Melba came to Salinas and we drove my car to Las Vegas because one needs a car there. Melba could not win playing the slots while Mom was doing very well. At one casino, Mom told Melba to play a certain machine but Melba refused so Mom played it and hit a good jackpot. Money fell from the machine filling the tray underneath. What we have learned about slots was that if Melba had played that machine, she may not have won. We took a day off from gambling to sight see. One attraction was the Ethel M Candy Factory located on the East side of the Boulder Highway in the city of Henderson Nevada. We toured the factory, getting free samples of the candy, then visited their very large cactus garden. My mother is always attracted to any kind of flower so naturally we spent time visiting the garden. As I understand it, they have every variety of cacti that grows in the Southwest United States and some tropical countries. Since we had been there before, the love of my life acted as tour guide for my mother showing her the different cacti and pointed out the one that we have in our yard and others that would grow in our area.

When it was time to go to the Grand Canyon it was a very windy day although it was hot. The flight was somewhat uneventful until we arrived at the Grand Canyon. As part of the tour, the pilots fly down into the canyon, make a sharp turn around and proceed to the airfield. When our pilots performed this feat, the plane dropped about a hundred feet straight down. Melba and Mom shouted, "Oh Lord we are going to die". Everyone on the plane was nervous and was glad then the plane landed.

There was a railing to prevent people from going too close to the edge of the canyon. Mom saw a flower that she liked and crawled under the railing and climbed out on the ledge to picked the flower. Nobi yelled to me to get Mom before she fell. After pulling her back to safety, we asked her if she knew that it was a mile to the bottom of the canyon and that it was a good thing that the ranger did not see her. Other than this incident we had a good time there as well as a nice dinner at the lodge. We stayed there two days seeing the sights. On the trip back to Las Vegas, it was a nice day so the trip back was without incident.

The love of my life was beginning to get tired of working but did not want to just quit. She wanted to receive some type of retirement pay since she had worked a long time. She soon found out that if she worked one more year she could retire with pay. At the same time I was getting tired of commuting to San Mateo. I knew that I would not work long enough to get retirement money from this job, so I could retire too any time I wanted. I was already receiving retirement pay from the Army and we had saved and invested our money so we had quite a nest egg put away. I just walked into the boss's office and told him that I was going to retire and did.

During the year that Nobi had to work before retiring, I was home so she had me watching and reporting on soap operas (now called day time dramas). I got so depressed because I stayed in bed while my wife went to work and because I had to watch the d**n soaps. One day after reading the daily newspaper, I looked in the want ads and was delighted that someone wanted a data processing manager. I jumped out of bed, went to my desk and found an old resume, cut out the want ad from the paper and taped it to the resume and mailed it. I immediately felt better. I could not honestly say that I wanted a job, but I was offered the job and decided to give it three years. After Nobi retired, I still had two more years before we would be free as birds to travel as we saw fit.

Chapter 19

MORE OF OUR TRAVELS

During the two year period I worked at Gentry Foods and after Nobi retired we only went on short bus trips mostly with Lee Berta Tours to places like Reno over the weekends and holidays. Sometimes we went to visit our children at their homes during the same weekends and holidays. Just as the two years was ending, the owners decided to sell the company to a larger firm located next door. This was just fine with me because now I did not have the stress of quitting. I had been instrumental to the successful operation of the company during my three year tenure; however I was not eligible for any retirement so the management decided that they would award me with a year's salary. We put most of the money in the bank and decided to take a trip with the rest. Before we had planned our trip, the new owners, who had let me come to work for three months with nothing to do but sit around, decided at the last minute that they should transfer selected data from our computers and reformat this data to their computers. To accomplish this, they hired me as a consultant paying me much more than my regular salary.

    When my work was completed, Nobi and I decided to visit my sister Melba who lived in Omaha, Nebraska. We decided that we would take our time driving because now we had the rest of our lives to ourselves. Our first three days we spent in Reno at the casinos. Our luck, which is Nobi's luck, brought us seven hundred dollars as she won the top prize on a nickel machine. My babe wanted to bring this money back home if we could so it was tucked away where we could not get to it, unless we really needed it. We left Reno after our three days were up and travelled to Wendover, Nevada which borders with

Utah. We stopped here because this was our last chance to play in casinos until we returned. We only stayed overnight because our luck was missing so we just had a nice dinner and went to bed in order to get an early start the next morning.

We continued our journey early because I wanted to travel through Utah and on into Wyoming before stopping. It was our custom to start looking for a motel about three o'clock in the afternoon so that we did not want to get too tired because we believed that is when accidents happen. We also stopped along the way for food and gas when necessary but also if anything interesting came along, we would stop to take a look. When the time we normally stopped arrived, we were at Laramie, Wyoming. We pulled into the motel that we chose to spend the night. After we registered, Nobi decided to walk to the room which was just a few steps from the office. I said that I would bring the car closer to make unloading our bags easier. As I started the car, smoke suddenly poured through from under the hood. I jumped out and opened the hood to see that our car was on fire. I rushed into the office and borrowed their fire extinguisher and put out the blaze. I then called AAA and asked for a tow truck which came in due time. The driver asked me where I wanted him to take my car for repair. I told him that I had no idea and would leave it up to him. He took my car to a shop that looked more like a junk yard than a repair shop but the tow truck driver assured me that the shop operators were good. When we told the operator what was wrong with my car, he did not say anything but turned and went back to his shop while we waited in the tow truck. He was gone for such a long time that I began to worry that he was not going to service my car. I did notice that there was a lot of activity moving cars around in the shop area but did not understand it at the time. When the operator did return, he told us that he had to make room for my car and that his crew would work on it immediately. I was sure glad to hear that. He did tell me that I was lucky because the fire did not burn the harness that provides electricity to everything electrical in the car including the lights and due to the cars age, he would have trouble getting another one which could take days. He then told me that my car would be ready in about two hours. At this time the tow truck driver placed my car where the operator wanted it and left the scene. I had nothing else to do for the two hours so I went walking around the neighborhood of the shop. As I walked around I came upon a bar but when I looked into the window I thought I would have trouble with the patrons so I did not go in. Finding nothing else interesting to do, I decided to return to the bar and if I had trouble, then I would address it. My fears were misplaced because I met the friendliest bunch of guys who bought my first beer. When asked why I was in town, I told them about my car and they assured me that my car was in the best of hands. The two hours went fast because I was having such a good time in the bar. I went back to the garage and sure enough my car was ready and the bill for the repair was much less than I anticipated. These guys also packed up all the defective parts and gave me a written statement indicating why the parts failed as these same parts were installed on my car at the beginning of our trip. When I got home I had no trouble getting Firestone to make everything right.

The next morning the love of my life and I continued on our journey. We stopped for breakfast about 9:00 AM at which time I realized that we were not going to make it all the way to Omaha before dark; and since I did not know the way to my sister Melba's house I saw no reason to hurry so we travelled slower than normal during this leg of the trip. In the late afternoon, we stopped in a small town just west of Lincoln called Aurora. At the motel we learned that they had a museum depicting how the pioneers lived and with nothing else to do we went to see it. We looked and examined things there until closing time when they kicked us out. The next morning we drove to Omaha and arrived before noon. I still had no idea how to get to my sister's house except to follow the street on which she lived until we got to her address. I knew that she lived on 40th street so I took the freeway exit nearest this street and began to follow it through the city. This was going to take a long time since we were on South 40th and she lived on North 40th. Still I had no other alternative so we continued our northward trek going around obstructions that blocked our way until we finally arrived on North 40th street and found her address. Melba and Harry, her husband was so surprised to see us. We spent the next five days touring around Omaha. There are only a couple of things that I remember of this trip. One is that Nobi and I met Melba's children and grandchildren, other than the two that lived in Little Rock, for the first time. The other was how amazing the two year old daughter of Patrice was at the time. That little child could talk about anything and everything. I tried to play a little trick on her by telling her to go sit in her grandfather's lap and ask him to give you a dollar and when he gives it to you, come back and we would split it. She did as I instructed but when she came back to me, she said no on the splitting of the money. I took her by the hand and we went to the candy store about a block or so away and bought her anything she wanted there. It was not until we went to Omaha on the occasion of Melba's fiftieth wedding anniversary that I received my share of the dollar we scammed out of Harry.

Our next trip was with Lee Berta Tours on a bus trip to see the monument at Mount Rushmore where four of our presidents are sculptured in stone in the Black Hills of South Dakota. We had taken several short trips with her tour company and had come to be very familiar with her. On the trip I had the job of tending the bar. This was a bus trip, however she would only take twenty five passengers so that we could move freely about the bus. There were many stops along the way and at night we were boarded in hotels/motels so it was really not a bad way of travelling. Of course our first stop was at Reno Nevada and then on to Wendover which is on the border with Utah. It was here that our bus driver, named "Red", who we all knew and loved got sick. Seemed as though he had let his blood sugar get too low and almost went into a diabetic coma. Another bus had to come and take us on to Salt Lake City because that was where our hotel accommodations were for that night. We spent the next two days touring around Salt

Lake City. Nobi and I took the city tour along with some of the others in our group. We also went to visit the Mormon Tabernacle Choir Auditorium. The acoustics there are so great that from standing at the rear of the auditorium, two people whispering can be heard clearly. When we were ready to leave, "Red" had gotten his blood sugar under control and rejoined the group as our driver. The trip took us along the Grand Tetons where we stopped several times for picture taking and then on to Jackson Hole Wyoming. We spent two nights there which gave us one whole day of touring the city. I remember a park where the gate portal was made of elk antlers. Jackson Hole is a ski resort and since it was during the summer months that we visited, not much was happening.

The next morning we journeyed on to our next stop of Yellowstone National Park where we spent the next two nights. The tour company had hired a guide who took us in our own bus to all of the sights, including "Old Faithful Geyser". While we were there it did erupt on time spewing steam and hot water high into the air. I was able to get pictures, only from inside the lodge because we were eating lunch when it erupted. Yellowstone had had a major fire about six months before we arrived but the place where the fire burned had begun to regain its green color and small trees had begun to grow. We asked the park rangers what they had to do to put out the fire and were surprised to know they did nothing. They let the fire burn itself out. We also went to an area of the park where there were high water falls and yellow rock from which the park got its name. Back at the geyser area we were warned not to get off of the wooden walkway and not to be tempted to touch small pools of water no matter how inviting it looked because the water there was so hot it would take your skin and flesh off your bones. When it was time to leave we travelled on to the Black Hills of South Dakota passing through Sturgis where motorcycle groups gather once per year; and then on to Deadwood where we had lodging. We had heard that Deadwood had many casinos, but there was really only two. The others were stores with a few slot machines. I was able to video tape anything here without having my camera confiscated. Nobi and I ventured through some of the so called casinos without any luck so we went along the street until we came upon a stage show just beginning so I videotaped the whole thing. I found out that many of our group missed this when we reviewed my tapes on the bus during our return trip. There was a place that claimed that it was where Jesse James was killed. The next morning we ventured on to Mount Rushmore National Monument where the heads of four of our presidents is carved on the mountain. On the way there we stopped to see the "Devils Tower" a place where volcanic action caused a mountain several thousand feet to be pushed skyward. At Mount Rushmore we learned so much about how the heads of George Washington, Thomas Jefferson, Abraham Lincoln and Theodore Roosevelt were carved into the mountain. I did not know that they made several smaller heads before carving the mountain. It really is a sight to see. Our final stop was to visit the rugged eroded layered rock deposits of the Badlands National Park, and to begin our trip home covering some of the same highways.

 Between major trips Nobi and I took several smaller trips to places like Reno, Carson City, Laughlin and Las Vegas. While most trips to Las Vegas were about the same, the one that stood out was when Robert and Barb met us there and Barb announced that she was pregnant. This pregnancy turned out to be our first granddaughter, Krista. Another time at Las Vegas was when The Las Vegas Hilton featured the Star Trek Experience. This was an exhibit of Star Trek memorabilia. We spent the whole day there viewing the various exhibits, taking a ride on the Enterprise Shuttle landing in the basement of the hotel and taking

SKY PRINCESS

pictures as members of the crew. Some of the trips were with Lee Berta Tours; others we went on our own or with other tour companies. Most of these short tours were to casinos because we liked to play the penny and nickel slots without losing too much of our money. We also joined groups like the "Active Seniors" that conducted guided tours to exciting places. Our first trip with Active Seniors was a cruise to Alaska with stops at Vancouver and Victoria British Columbia; Sitka and Anchorage Alaska. Syl and Lorraine from next door and Bert and Edie, Syl and Lorraine's brother/sister also went on the trip. The morning we were to depart was the day that Mrs. Devoe who lived on the other side of our house died. We felt awful bad that we could not stay and at least attend her funeral but all monies for the trip had been paid and it was too late to get any refund. This trip started by boarding a bus at the Active Senior's building and travelling to San Francisco where we boarded a Princess Cruise ship similar to the one that was featured on the television show, The Love Boat. After settling in our cabin we returned to the main deck to witness the departure of the ship from the harbor and especially see the ship pass under the Golden Gate Bridge. Right away we began to feed us because there was various sandwiches spread on a portion of the deck with a live band playing as we sampled the faire. Our first stop was Vancouver.

Our only choices of shore tours were either the city tour or the garden tour. The love of my life chose the garden tour so we spent the whole day touring various gardens of the city. Most were very beautiful and peaceful places. In the dining room on the ship, we were divided into five couple tables so that we would be able to get acquainted with strangers. Each couple was given a bottle of wine selected from the wine menu and could be consumed at any time during the trip. At our table I became the wine expert since no one else had any knowledge of wines. We decided that one couple each day would get their wine and the whole table would drink it. This worked well because we had wine with each evening meal throughout the cruise. After a few days on the cruise my love said that she wanted our whole family to go on a cruise together. Somehow we could never put together a time when we could all be free to go. She said that she would be willing to pay the initial cost for every member of the family, however I am sure that money was not the reason we could not make this happen for her. This is one of the few things that she wanted that I did not give her and maybe before my life is over, I will be able to get the family together and go on a cruise hoping that she would be with us in spirit. All in all, she was happy on this trip as we dressed up for dinner and afterwards went on the promenade deck for entertainment. There was a stage show almost every night. We went early so that we could get good seats. One thing about cruises is that there is always plenty of food. I bet I gained five pounds on this trip.

Our next adventure with the Active Seniors was a trip to Washington DC and Pennsylvania. It was very hard to leave on this trip because the night before we were to leave, Syl, our next door neighbor and our friend had suffered a heart attack and collapsed on the floor of his kitchen. On this particular night I was coming home from a meeting and saw the ambulance. I thought at the time that it was at my house, but when I pulled into my driveway I could see that the trouble was next door. Syl was taken to the hospital and died a few days later. Again, we had paid for the trip and it was too late to have our money refunded, so we had no other choice but to continue with our plans. We felt so bad because we wanted to be there for Lorraine because so often Syl had been there for us when I had to serve overseas. It always gave me comfort in knowing my family would be safe with Syl and Lorraine next door. From the Active Senior's building we took a bus to San Francisco where we boarded a plane to Baltimore. We had our own private bus that would take us to all of the places on our schedule. We first went to see the Liberty Bell and then to Independence Hall where a tall nice looking young man gave a great dissertation on the Declaration of Independence. He was able to show us the scratched up copy of the document written by Thomas Jefferson and how the Continental Congress argued over words and phrases until the final document was approved and was penned by

Timothy Matlock. Another place we went in Philadelphia was to visit the Carpenters Hall and to Betsy Ross' house. Before we left this area, we spent the whole day touring a battlefield where George Washington's army fought and visiting Amish Country and a small town called Intercourse. To show that you had been to such a place, the post office would post cancel a letter if you purchased an envelope and stamp. The next day we journeyed to Washington DC where we stayed at the Washington Hotel on Pennsylvania Avenue. Nobi and I had been here once before and had seen some of the things but had time to spend at some of the museums on the mall. We were driven back to Baltimore and boarded a plane for our flight home.

The next trip we took with the Active Seniors was to Disney World in Florida. We boarded a bus at the Active Seniors' building as usual, enroute to San Francisco airport for our flight to Orlando. After settling into our hotel we boarded a charter to Kissimmee to see a show about the Knights of the Round Table in old England. The audience was broken down into sections; each section was to root for their special knight. We were fed dinner before the show began, however no utensil were given so we had to eat with our hands breaking apart our game hen before eating it. It was really fun, but our knight lost during the first round. The next two days we spent at Disney World and EPCOT center. What words can I say about Disney World and EPCOT center that would give justice to the place? I will just put a picture gallery in the space below:

The final trip we took with the Active Seniors Group was to cruise around the San Juan Islands off the coast of Washington State near Seattle. We departed the Active Seniors building by bus to the San Francisco airport where we boarded a plane and flew to the Seattle/Tacoma airport. We had a charter bus that took us to the hotel in Seattle where we were to spend a couple of days touring around the city. After resting overnight at the hotel where we had our breakfast, our first adventure was to the Space Needle where we had our lunch at the restaurant at the top. My babe was a little apprehensive about riding the open (glass cage) elevator to such a high altitude, but I held her hand and she was alright. Upon arrival at the top we had to wait quite a while for a table because there was a long line and more than our group was there. When we finally were seated; we were lucky to get a table near the windows; we saw that the entire restaurant was revolving so our view was always changing. This made our lunch so much more enjoyable. Of course there was the elevator ride back down to the ground where lots of souvenirs were on sale. I do not believe we bought much, maybe a post card or two to send to our family back home.

The next day we went to the boat, but first we moved to a hotel near the place the boat was docked. We had about an hour to put our things in our rooms and then off to the boat. It was not a large boat, nothing like a cruise ship however there were only about 25 of us. We were to eat our breakfast and supper on land and have our lunch on the boat. Our boat was called the Viking Star, a 58 foot twin diesel boat which was large enough for us to move around freely. In addition to the main deck, there was an area upstairs near the place where the captain steered the boat. On board was a young college age girl who was hired to serve us drinks and at lunch time, our lunch. She was such a lovely girl who was very friendly and everyone just loved and cared for her.

We had heard from the captain that sometimes wild animals could be sighted along the bank so some of us were on the top deck looking to see if we could spot a bear or something. Our young waitress came up to serve the captain a drink or something. The steps leading down to the main cabin were a pole stairs, meaning that the steps were very narrow near the pole and got wider over near the wall. I happen to be standing at the top of the steps near the pole, as I looked to the banks for wild animals. Our young waitress started down the stairs and I thought that she was too near the pole so I made her go around me toward the wall where the steps were wider. A little later I also decided to go back down and join my sweetheart who was talking to some of the other ladies on the main deck. Guess what! I forgot to use the wide portion of the stairs and about half way down, I fell all the way to the bottom. I put my hands out to break my fall and when I got up, all of my fingers were bent back. I just took my other hand and turned them back down; however, the tendons in my little finger of my right hand were torn loose so I could not bend it. When the captain heard of my fall, he was worried that I was going to sue him because he had heard about California people being sue happy. I did not see this at first because I was nursing my hand, but others in our group saw how unhappy he looked. When I learned of this, I went up and sat in the seat next to him. Right away he asked me what I intended to do about my accident. I told him that I was not going to do anything because it was my own fault. I knew about the stairs and told him about my actions with the waitress, therefore I knew there was danger. His demeanor immediately changed and he told me to come up and sit and talk anytime.

After we had cruised around the islands for three days; we were taken by ferry boat to a larger island where we were treated to a salmon dinner; prepared by Indians over an open flame on a spit made from small branches. The meal was very good and was served very fast considering we had to wait for each salmon to be cooked as they were not cooked ahead of being served. After we were stuffed, we took the ferry back to Seattle.

On our last full day we boarded a charter bus to go on what was termed as the scenic circle. We passed many picturesque places along the way but the most memorable was a Scandinavian village at a small town I believe to be Leavenworth. This village is similar to Solvang in California, just north of Santa Barbara, only larger. My description of the place will not do it justice, so I will just give you pictures.

After my father died my sweetheart and I made annual trips to Little Rock, Arkansas to visit my mother. We would leave home very early in the morning and travel to Barstow where we would spend the night. Early the next morning we travelled along Interstate 40 until we reached the cutoff to Laughlin, Nevada. There we would check in to a hotel (mostly without cost because we were members of their players club) for three or four days playing penny slots and generally having a good time. When it was time to leave, we would go across the river into Arizona and take a back road to Kingman where we picked up Interstate 40 again with would eventually get to Little Rock. After making this trip several years, we started to look for Indian casinos where we could spend the night and have something to do during the evening before going to bed. Because we began each day early in the morning, we would stop for the day around three o'clock. We found a casino at Grants, New Mexico, a small town just before Albuquerque, and another at Clinton, Oklahoma, a small town before reaching Oklahoma City.

Travelling along Interstate 40 just over the Arkansas/Oklahoma border there is a diamond mine where one can dig for diamonds. For a fee of $10.00 one can dig a large bucket of the soil and rock from the mine and sift through it. If you find a diamond it is yours to keep. Of course we did not know any of this until we saw it on television after we had stopped going on this journey because of the death of my mother.

Thereafter we only travelled on short trips, either to see our children who lived approximately 140 miles away; to Chukchansi which is located about 30 miles north of Fresno; or to Palace Casino at Lemoore which is about 25 miles west of Visalia. When visiting Robert, Barbara and the grandchildren, we often visited the Chumash Casino at Santa Ynez. When visiting Judy there are several casinos we could visit around Sacramento. We could not venture far from home because my dear wife's health was beginning to fail.

Chapter 20

ROBERT AND BARBARA'S SILVER ANNIVERSARY

Our son and daughter-in-law celebrated their 25th wedding anniversary on August 10, 2010. About three weeks or so before the celebration, my granddaughter called us on the phone and invited us to a surprise celebration of her parent's silver wedding anniversary. I promised her that we would help her with the cost because we knew it would be more than she and her brother could afford. On the morning of the celebration, Nobi and I met our daughter Judy at the hotel located in the town next to their town. Since the celebration was a surprise, we could not be seen, or they would know something was happening. We went to a Wal-Mart there but to sure we were not seen, we went up and down each row of the parking lot looking for their car. Having made sure that they were not shopping there that day, it was alright for us to go in. Judy purchased a poker set that was on sale so we went back to the hotel and played three handed poker. Judy and I knew the rules much better than Nobi and were much more confident that we were going to win. I am sorry to say that Nobi kicked our butts, taking all of our chips causing us to get more chips from the bank. As we were playing, my honey said that she had to go to the bathroom so as Judy and I waited, we heard a noise coming from the bathroom. We discovered that Nobi had tried to get up from the commode and fell onto the bath tub hard enough to render her unconscious. It was good that Judy's police training (she was retired from the police force due to injury) made her much more level headed and more in control.

I immediately tried to call 911 but could not get the phone to work. Judy on the other hand placed a cold towel on her face until she regained consciousness. She said that she was alright but I was still shaky.

On the night of the party we were all assembled on the patio of the selected restaurant. My granddaughter Krista had a hard time getting her parents to come to the restaurant and a harder time in getting them to sit on the patio. After much pleading with them, they finally agreed to come out on the patio where we really surprised them. The party was very nice. Krista did a fine job in selecting the place the party was held. Everyone ordered what they wanted to eat and drink from the menu and a fine time was held by all.

Since we no longer had to hide from them, we went to their home after the party for a while, but returned to the hotel for the night. Judy had to go home the next morning but Nobi and I stayed with Robert and Barbara for a couple more days since we had no obligations.

Chapter 21

THE LAST OF...

As Nobi's health began to fail, the doctors informed us that there was nothing more they could do as the Chemo was no longer effective against her cancer. Her body was producing more Myeloma cells than red blood cells causing her to become weaker. My babe was confined to a wheel chair and I had to help her with almost everything she wanted to do. I did not mind taking care of her because I loved her more than anything on this earth. If I could have, I would have changed places with her.

Trip to Las Vegas—Our last trip to Las Vegas was during the month of May 2010. It was rather cold and wet from rain. Nobi knew that her time on this earth was running out and wanted to take her last trip there. When she asked me to make reservations for our trip I wondered if she could endure a ten day trip because we always went to Laughlin for a few days before going to Las Vegas. To assure myself that the long drive would not wear her down, I scheduled an overnight stop at Barstow. When we arrived at Laughlin and were assigned our room, I made her take a short nap before going down to the casino to play. I never let her get out of the wheel chair unless we were in our room. Everything went well during our stay there because of the precautions I had taken. When we left Laughlin driving the 100 miles to Las Vegas, we took our time so that she would remain calm and not get tired. At Las Vegas, we normally stopped at the grocery store to buy food to make our breakfast each morning. We were surprised to learn that our favorite store had closed so we had to look for another before going to our timeshare hotel.

The second day there it rained so we stayed close to our hotel. This meant going across the street to Planet Hollywood Casino. The rain had stopped temporarily so we ventured next door to Paris Casino which has indoor passage to Bally's. This meant that we could play in three casinos without too much trouble as I had to push Nobi's wheel chair wherever we went. After we had played in Bally's and Paris, it had started to rain again. We put the hoods up on our jackets and braved the rain the short distance back to Planet Hollywood. On the way, there was a metal moving escalator that looked inviting and a short cut to the entrance so I decided to use it. Unfortunately I did not lock the wheels on the wheel chair before getting on the thing so instead of moving the wheel chair up the ramp, the wheels began to spin and I fell down and the wheel chair backed over me pinning me to the moving metal base cutting into both of my knees. Two really nice people noted my situation and held the wheels preventing them from spinning, causing the wheel chair to go up the ramp. I was able to get up and help them to the top. My knees were cut very badly and my pants torn but we made it back to the hotel. We finished our seven days there without further incident and spent two more days in the area of Whisky Pete's; then made our trip back home to Salinas.

Thanksgiving Day—As Thanksgiving drew near, my sweetheart told me that this year there would be no cooking done on Thanksgiving Day. Normally our daughter Judy, a certified chef, comes and makes lots of Hors d'oeuvres and other dishes. Nobi told me to order from the super market everything we needed for our meal and if necessary order two complete meals. It was alright if the meats and other hot dishes were warmed, but no one would be tied down in the kitchen working on the meal. I think Judy enjoys making the meals for our family on holidays and looks forward to it. She looked disappointed when I told her that her mother did not want any cooking this year. Nobi also told me that there would be no football or other sports on television and that we would sit together as a family and visit all of that day. The boys did not understand this either buy they complied, somewhat. When all was said and done, we had a wonderful holiday.

Christmas—As Christmas drew near I received the same instructions in regard to the Christmas dinner as I received for Thanksgiving. Everything would be bought already prepared. Judy was less disappointed and understood that her mother wanted us to visit as a family. We began our Christmas Day by having our breakfast.

Allowance was made for cooking breakfast so Judy and I prepared a nice meal. After breakfast we opened our presents (all wrapped presents were brought unopened to our home). Again no football was ordered but the boys slipped into the bedroom to check on the scores. We had invited our pastor and his wife, George and Isomi Doyal, for dinner. One of my presents was a large poker set complete with chips and cards. After dinner we placed together two tables on our patio and we all played poker with very loose rules because Isomi Doyal did not know how to play and the love of my life was so weak that she needed help. If Isomi or Nobi called their hand wrong, someone would reevaluate the hand and call it correctly and if it won, they would take the pot. We all had a very good time until darkness came upon us and we had to discontinue the game.

New Years—Normally we do not have any special activity for New Year's Day, however my dear wife wanted to have black eyed peas, corn bread, and ham. There is an old southern folk tale about this meal bringing good luck if eaten on New Year's Day. I cooked it for her and she seemed to enjoy it. After the meal was over and I had cleaned up, I came into the family room where she was lying down on the couch and said to her, "Honey it has been a long time since I told you that I love you, as I have been so busy." Without hesitation, she answered, "yes, but you show your love for me every day".

Casino trip—It was a few days after the New Year that my wife said that she wanted to go to Tachi Palace Casino and Chukchansi Casino, a five day trip. My common sense told me that she was too weak for such a trip. I tried to reason with her that I did not believe she would survive the trip but she began to cry and say that she wanted to go. The love that I have for this woman took over my good common sense and I began to weaken by saying that I would take her if each of the casinos had a unisex restroom where I could take her if needed while on the casino floor. I called each one and to my surprise each did have such a restroom so I made reservations. I still had doubts everything would go well and we would have a good time. The trip to the first casino is at Lemoore about 150 miles away and was travelled without incident. Upon arrival, we were assigned a room immediately so I had her take a short nap and rest before I took her on the casino floor. After her nap, I put her in her wheel chair and we went down to the casino. To my surprise she did have a good time. Late in the afternoon I made her go back to the room and rest before having our dinner.

I let her play for a while after dinner and when I could see that she was tired took her to the room for the night. The next morning we had a nice breakfast and since she appeared rested we again went to the casino and played. I watched her closely for signs that she was getting tired so that I could act immediately. I have to admit I was not having fun because of worry about her. I also have to admit that I was acting like a mother hen with her chicks. We spent the two days we had reserved and on the morning of the third I was surprised and pleased that everything went better than I had hoped as we departed for Chukchansi. She slept in the car during the journey and I was happy that she was resting. Again we were lucky to be assigned a room as soon as we arrived, especially since it was still morning because most of the rooms were still being cleaned. I thought it would be alright for her to go directly to the casino as soon as I had taken our bags and things to our room. We played until the noon hour when we went to the buffet for our lunch. She told me that she wanted to eat a large salad so I helped her put on her salad the dishes that she wanted. After she finished eating the salad she wanted stir fried vegetables so I got that for her and she ate that too. I was pleased that she was eating well. In the afternoon I made her rest because I could see that she became tired much sooner after resting and I began to worry more. On the second day she spent more time in bed than on the casino floor. We had reserved three days there so I went to the front desk and asked if there was a penalty to pay if we went home early and was assured that no penalty was due. As we were preparing for bed I told her we were going home tomorrow and began to get our bags together. She immediately began to cry that she wanted to stay. This was the first time I had talked sharply to her in many years, but I said no, we were going home. I felt bad about refusing her but I had to stick to it. I said to her, "Honey I am afraid, if anything happens to you I will not know what to do; I do not know the medical situation here and if you should die, how will I get your body home; No! We are going home." She did not like it, but accepted it. The next morning we departed for home. When we arrived home, as I was helping her into the house, she told me that I was right, that she doubted that she could have survived another day there.

A few days later my sweetheart became so weak that she could not stand alone, or go to the bathroom even with help so I brought the "port—a-potty" into our bedroom and told her doctor that I could no longer take care of her without professional help. Her doctor said that she would send the visiting nurses. A nurse came later that day to start a case file and to bring the necessary supplies that I would need for her care. I also notified our children that they should be prepared to come home as their mother was nearing the end of her life. On this day our pastor paid her a visit and asked her if there was anything about her religion that she wanted to know. She told him no, she was okay with that. He also asked her if there was anything that she wanted to know about dying and she told him that she was okay with that too. Her Last Meal—Nobi asked me to prepare for her supper stir-fried vegetables over rice. I had some thinly sliced beef so I stir fried this first and removed it from the pan. After cutting the vegetables I stir fried these then returned the beef to the pan and added oyster sauce. The rice was cooking as I made the vegetables so when all was ready; I placed a tray on her side of the bed and another by my side. As I placed her food on her tray I saw that she could not pick up her fork so I stayed and fed her. She said that it was very good. After she had finished, I went on my side to eat my dinner and as I did so, we talked. I finished my meal and took the dishes into the kitchen and returned to bed. I held her in my arms as we continued to talk until we both went to sleep. The next morning I could not awake her and noticed that her eyes were a dark gray. I realized then that she had slipped into a coma sometime during the night. Our children also came home that day. I notified her doctor of the situation and she said that she would cancel the visiting nurses and would send hospice to me.

Her last days alive—When the hospice nurses arrived, they informed us that we could only make her comfortable; as much as possible for as long as she survived. All of our children and grandchildren had arrived to be with her during her last days even though she was not aware of any of us. The hospice nurse gave us three small bottles of medicine and instructions on the use of each. My daughter Judy took charge in administering the medicine and made forms on the computer so that no mistakes would be made in administering the medicine. We all took turns being with her, making sure that she was resting and not in distress. We all had hopes that she would come out of the coma and return to normal as she had done so many times before. This hope made my children think that they could return home to their normal lives. James, who lives in the area, had returned home. Robert, Barbara and the grandchildren had also departed for home. We had hired a woman with nurse training to come at various times of the day to help me administer the medicine; help keep her clean; and to re-position her in the bed to prevent bed sores. We could have saved ourselves this trouble because at 9:30 PM this very night, January 21, 2011 the love of my life succumbed to death. My daughter Judy and I had checked on her a few minutes before and she was still alive but when Judy looked in on her she called me and told me that she was gone. Robert, Barbara and the grandchildren had just arrived home and had to return immediately. The hospice nurse returned and confirmed that she had died and fixed the time of death. This nurse had us round up all of her medicine which she destroyed. She instructed us to wait at least an hour before calling the mortuary of our choice to remove Nobi's body.

Although we knew that the love of my life was now in her heavenly home, we were stunned over our loss. We sat around in our family room unable to discuss the necessary things that we needed to do, or to go to bed since it was very late in the night. Later, we finally went to bed but did not sleep very well. The next morning, after breakfast, we planned her funeral. We decided that we would have a private burial ceremony, inviting only family and close friends and the next day have a public memorial service. With the memorial service bulletin, we gave to each guest a card purchased from the mortuary, that I thought was appropriate. It read: "God saw you getting tired and a cure was not to be. So he put his arms around you and whispered, "Come to me". With tearful eyes we watched you pass away. Although we loved you dearly, we could not make you stay. A golden heart stopped beating, hard working hands at rest. God broke our hearts to prove to us, He only takes the best."

Chapter 22

LOVE BEYOND THE GRAVE

It has been eight months since the love of my life departed this earth. Although I have had some good days most of my time I feel as if I am in a fog feeling that nothing is real. I am enrolled in two different group grief counsel sessions. One meets at 1:00 PM on Wednesdays at a large church. The other meet at 4:00 PM Thursdays at the Cancer Center, both are in my home town of Salinas, California. As of this writing, I have not disposed of any of her clothing or any of her other things. I find it comforting to visit her grave site often because somehow I feel closer to her as I polish and clip the grass around the headstone.

One day as I was eating my breakfast, I was facing the china cabinet where we kept the good glassware, china and silver ware along with other pieces that we put away to prevent them from being broken. My thoughts immediately were that we did not enjoy these things while my sweetheart was alive and now we would never enjoy them together with our family. We did not use them even for our Thanksgiving or Christmas dinner as a family. As I peered into the cabinet, I remembered back to one Thanksgiving when we were having our extended family members dining with us, I asked her if we should use the good china. She told me, "No some pieces might get broken". I jokingly asked her if we were waiting for the President of the United States to have dinner with us. That brought just one of "those" looks. As I continued looking into the cabinet, my pain grew and grew until tears filled my eyes and I had to leave the table. I prayed to God to let Nobi come to me and if that was not possible to allow me to come to her. As I lay on the bed praying, tears streamed down my cheeks. After I pulled myself together and dried my tears, I finished my breakfast and had a somewhat nice day.

God must have been very busy because nothing happened during the next three days. I went to bed early on the night of the third day because I wanted to read. I was amused by the shenanigans of Spenser and Hawk, characters in the book by Robert B. Parker that I was reading. I had just turned out the light and turned over in the bed when my I felt the presence of another person in the room. I turned on the light and look around but saw no one. When I turned out the light again, my arm was drawn to a place on Nobi's side of the bed. There was a pulsating sensation in my right hand that felt like a beating heart. Of course I thought that I was making this sensation with my own body or I was imagining it. I felt different places in the bed, all on her side, but did not feel anything but the sheet on the bed. It was only the one spot that I felt the beating heart.

My first thought was to keep this event to myself because I did not want anyone to think that I had "jumped off of the deep end", but on the other hand I could not forget what had happened to me. I also did not fully understand the significance of it either. My grief counsel group meeting was being held the next evening so I went early to the meeting hoping that the counselor would also be early. Luck was with me so I had a short private meeting with him. He told me that God could do anything and that it really did appear that the love of my life had indeed visited me and let me know that still had her heart. This gave me confidence to share my experience with the rest of the group. A group discussion of my experience led others to reveal similar experiences. I would like to share the experiences of others in the group; however we vowed not to repeat anything that is revealed in group session.

It has been almost a year since my sweetheart's death and I am still grieving. Yet I have made a plan for the rest of my life. The first thing I will do, with God's help is to forgive those Army Officers that I feel was responsible for injustices done to me. In order to get on with my life, I know that I will need female companionship; however I will not have a serious relationship. I hope to find a woman who has had a long and happy marriage similar to the one that I had. We will mutually agree to keep our former spouses in the uppermost part of our minds and will be able to discuss our feelings for them freely without jealousness or the feeling of competing with them. There will be no intimacy, other than the holding of hands and friendly hugs. I know that I am describing a friend here, but for the lack of the proper word, I choose to call her my super friend and travelling companion.

Ever since my darling wife came to visit me that night I have had almost no fear of dying. I will not do anything to speed the event, but I am looking forward to it because I know that the love of my life is in her heavenly home waiting for me. I cannot know how things will be there; whether we will be young, old, or somewhere in between. I do not know even if we will have bodies, but I will not care as long as I am allowed to spend eternity with her.

Grief counsel has taught me that love does not stop when one partner dies. I loved her with all of my heart every day since I met her and will continue to love her after we are together in eternity.

www.ingramcontent.com/pod-product-compliance
Lightning Source LLC
LaVergne TN
LVHW091546060526
838200LV00036B/731